# spells
## for
# good times

© Connie Wurster

## About the Author

Kerri Connor has been practicing her craft for over thirty-five years and has run an eclectic Pagan family group, The Gathering Grove, since 2003.

She is a frequent contributor to Llewellyn annuals and is the author of *Wake, Bake & Meditate: Take Your Spiritual Practice to a Higher Level with Cannabis* and *420 Meditations*. Kerri runs The Spiral Labyrinth, a mini spiritual retreat, at her home in Ringwood, IL.

RITUALS, SPELLS, AND MEDITATIONS TO
BOOST CONFIDENCE + POSITIVITY

*spells*
*for*
*good times*

*kerri connor*

WITH KRYSTLE HOPE

LLEWELLYN PUBLICATIONS | WOODBURY, MINNESOTA

FIRST EDITION
First Printing, 2022

Book design by Christine Ha
Cover design by Cassie Willett
Runes chart on page 194 by the Llewellyn Art Department

Llewellyn Publications is a registered trademark of Llewellyn Worldwide Ltd.

**Library of Congress Cataloging-in-Publication Data**
Names: Connor, Kerri, author.
Title: Spells for good times : rituals, spells & meditations to boost
    confidence & positivity / Kerri Connor.
Description: First edition. | Woodbury, Minnesota : Llewellyn Publications,
    2022. | Summary: "Featuring a variety of simple spells, rituals,
    affirmations, meditations, prayers, and journal prompts, this practical
    guide helps you and your community raise positive energy and look toward
    a brighter future"—Provided by publisher.
Identifiers: LCCN 2021058488 (print) | LCCN 2021058489 (ebook) | ISBN
    9780738770468 | ISBN 9780738770567 (ebook)
Subjects: LCSH: Incantations. | Charms. | Rites and ceremonies. | Magic.
Classification: LCC BF1558 .C6595 2022  (print) | LCC BF1558  (ebook) | DDC
    133.4/4—dc23/eng/20220201
LC record available at https://lccn.loc.gov/2021058488
LC ebook record available at https://lccn.loc.gov/2021058489

Llewellyn Worldwide Ltd. does not participate in, endorse, or have any authority or responsibility concerning private business transactions between our authors and the public.

All mail addressed to the author is forwarded but the publisher cannot, unless specifically instructed by the author, give out an address or phone number.

Any internet references contained in this work are current at publication time, but the publisher cannot guarantee that a specific location will continue to be maintained. Please refer to the publisher's website for links to authors' websites and other sources.

Llewellyn Publications
A Division of Llewellyn Worldwide Ltd.
2143 Wooddale Drive
Woodbury, MN 55125-2989
www.llewellyn.com

Printed in the United States of America

# Other Books by Kerri Connor

*For Laura and Wendy—the River Witches.*
*—Kerri*

*For Kahlen and River.*

*To Heather, Michelle, Jay, Kye, and Jasmin, who
always supported and encouraged me, and to my
mom for this opportunity.*
*—Krystle*

# Contents

## Chapter 5: Bedtime Routines  77

## Chapter 6: Workings for Self-Esteem  95

## Chapter 7: Magic for Coping  127

## Chapter 8: Shadow Work   151

## Chapter 9: Healing Others   179

# Introduction

Hello, friends, and welcome to a brighter future!

I am Kerri Connor, and this is my tenth book. I have been writing in the Pagan markets for twenty years and I am the High Priestess of The Gathering Grove, an earth-based spiritual/religious nonprofit organization in rural Illinois, north of Chicago. The Grove has been in existence since 2003, evolving over the years. My spiritual path began when I was sixteen years old and has taken many twists and turns through the world of Paganism over the past thirty-five years. I practice an eclectic brand of both witchcraft and Paganism.

Krystle Hope is my daughter. Unlike me, she was exposed to Paganism at a younger age and began walking her spiritual path at the age of eleven (when letters from Hogwarts are supposed to arrive). Krystle is both an active member of The Gathering Grove and the treasurer. She runs her own business, Crescent

Sapphire. Her two daughters have been raised in The Grove since birth, and she classifies herself as an eclectic Pagan witch.

We began writing this book coming out on the back side of the worst pandemic we have seen in our lifetimes. Vaccines are available and being put into arms as fast as they can in a race against mutating strains. Across the globe, people suffered the loss of loved ones, incomes, and homes. Many also lost confidence, sense of peace, and self-worth. Anxiety, insomnia, and depression have taken way too many prisoners.

Coupled with a nation that has suffered such terrible division that it led to an insurrection against our own capitol, many Americans felt another dose of helplessness kick in. We have watched and felt toxic energy multiply. Massive amounts of negative energy build up around us when we have tragedies on a grand scale, and we have suffered from several tragedies.

As witches, we need to work to turn that negative energy into positive energy, not only for ourselves but for our communities and the future. This means we need to take an active part in building a brighter future for ourselves, our families, our communities, and our planet. Any action, and often the most important action we can take, begins with ourselves. The work we do on and for ourselves shines a light onto others.

We can start this work right now. Today. We do not have to wait until January 1 to make resolutions if we want a better life. We don't have to wait to free up our schedule or complete just one more project. We can start a better, happier, brighter life any single moment we want. Anytime at all. Today sounds like a good enough day to us. How about you? Are you ready to start a new path to a happier life? Are you ready to feel better about yourself and the world around you? Are you ready to take back your own power and use it to give yourself the happiness you want and deserve?

We will use spells, rituals, affirmations, meditations, prayers, and journal writings along with other positive reinforcement measures to push away the gray, the low vibrations, the hate, the anger, and the fear, and instead send out high vibrations with love and positive energy. We know that our magic works best when we use it along with supporting work in the mundane world, and so this book is going to give plenty of ideas on how to do that too. We will focus on the positive as much as possible because, frankly, the negative has enjoyed too much of the limelight as it is. Let's promote love, happiness, and peace.

Now, don't get the wrong idea; we are fully aware that it's not all "Love and light make the world go 'round." That isn't the point here. The point is the world has suffered. The world has lost. Many people have found extreme common ground with recent historical events, which has let them know they are not alone. We have not only all felt pain, but we have also now recognized so much pain in others—more than we ever have in our lifetime until now. For empaths, the past several years have been absolutely overwhelming. We have the opportunity to use what we have learned and what we have seen to make some major decisions about how we want our lives to be in the future. The choice is truly up to each and every one of us. We can focus on the hate and fear that is still prevalent in our society, or we can focus on love and compassion, both for ourselves and for others.

There are many different theories about when the official Age of Aquarius began (or begins, as a few theories don't claim it is yet here). I am on the boat that the Great Conjunction, which took place in Aquarius on the Winter Solstice 2020, was the kickoff to this awesome new era. An Aquarius myself, this theory feels the truest to me. I have felt incredible energy shifts not only in the environment around me, but in myself too. This is our time. The world we want to create, we can. We can have equality for all. We can have peace. We can create a society that values all life. We can create a society that values love and compassion and wisdom. But we must do the work to get there. It won't happen overnight, and it will most certainly not be easy. Nothing worth having is. It will take work from all of us to create a more loving, more equitable future for all. We must be the beacons to light up the way.

There is a great awakening happening. People are opening their eyes and seeing the old ways don't necessarily mean the right ways. Things are changing, and with these changes come some issues, including not everyone changing. Not everyone wants a world filled with positivity and compassion. They do not want a world with equality. They still want a world with power and control resting in the hands of the few. Maybe, with any luck, some of our created positivity will reach those who appear to desperately need it. It's the most we can hope for. In some cases, people will leave our lives because they have not felt the awakening. In other cases, complete strangers will be drawn together by the energy this awakening radiates.

Creating a loving, compassionate world begins with each one of us. Learning how to heal, how to bounce back, how to move forward can be a difficult path. It is where the real work begins. This book is not a substitute for any situation that needs therapy. Magic should never be a replacement or substitute to therapy. It should always be in addition to the other work you do. We must always back up our magical work with work in the mundane world.

For those of you who are new to the Craft, the first chapter is an explanation of what magic is and how you can learn to use it to bring about a brighter future for yourself and others.

When the COVID-19 worldwide pandemic hit, jobs were lost, activities cancelled, and schools closed. Worlds turned upside down and people had no idea how to care for themselves when thrust into this nightmare. There are very few truly worldwide events, but the pandemic was a profound one with people all over the world suddenly experiencing very similar problems all at the same time.

Even with the terrible amount of loss, the COVID-19 pandemic gave us some important lessons. It taught us we must take care of ourselves. We simply cannot survive if we do not put more effort into caring for ourselves. It taught us our mental, emotional, and spiritual health is just as important as our physical health—not only our individual health and selves, but also as a society. It taught us if we do not care for one another, if we do not protect one another, we cannot survive as a society. And to learn this, we had to stay away from each other—often away from those we love the most. How ironic.

We hope this book will lift your spirits, open your eyes where needed, and inspire you. The old saying is all too true—life is short. And it's way too short to not spend it being the happiest you can be.

We are here to guide you and help show you the future is bright. You better grab your shades.

# 1
# Witchy Basics

I f you are new to magic, you most likely have a lot of questions. That's okay! We are going to start off with some basics that will have you on your way in no time at all. Even if you aren't new to magic, stick with us for this brief introduction to the Craft; you may still pick up something new to you.

The number one question people often want to know is what is magic? I have a definition I have used since 1986, and it works well for me. Magic is the intentional transformation of energy (not explained by current science). Everything around us is energy. Energy is the combination of vibration and information. Sometimes we can see it; sometimes we can't. When we cast spells, or even say a prayer, we are encouraging the energies of the universe to transform our wish into reality.

Let's think about it in scientific terms. We know that ice (a solid) vibrates slowly because it is a solid. The information it contains is water that is really cold. We can apply heat to the ice, and it will melt to water (a liquid) that vibrates more quickly. It is still water, but now it isn't as cold. If we apply more heat to the water, it will steam and break apart into the gases hydrogen and oxygen with very fast vibrations. We have transferred the energy of both hydrogen and oxygen by applying the energy of heat.

Magic works in a similar way. We transform energies with our intention to create a new reality. We have several different types of energies we can choose from or, for best results, combine to support our intention.

## Energy

Energy is all around us. It is in everything that surrounds us. It runs through us, and we, too, are a part of energy. Different parts of our world and existence consist of different types of energy. We can tap into these different types of energies to use in our magic.

There are four major types of energy that exist. Different traditions may teach different classifications of energies or the type of energies in those classifications. The following is the method I use, particularly when discussing generalities. If you are part of a specific tradition, feel free to use energy the way your tradition teaches, but don't skip over this section. You may find something you like, and it never hurts to learn how others work their magic.

The first type of energy is your own personal life force. Everything about you is energy. Both your physical and your spiritual bodies consist of this energy. It is the energy you have the most control over and therefore can use and direct the most effectively once you learn how. If you work with chakras, auras, or channels in the body, these are all a part of your own personal life force. We decide if we want to share our energies with others or not and can put up protective energetic barriers if needed. Think about how your energy affects others without you even really trying. A smile to someone who needs it, and you can feel their spirits raise. A stern, angry, hard stare can give someone goosebumps and make their hair stand on end. These are simple forms of energy we give off without even thinking about it. What can we do, then, when we really put our mind and our energy to it?

The next type of energy comes from the earth. There are several energy types that fall into the earth energy category. The first type can be felt through ley lines and sacred sites. Sacred sites include places such as famous henges, springs, or wells, but also include the sacred sites you create yourself. At The Gathering Grove, we have a few sacred sites: The Inner Grove Ritual Area, The Outer Grove Community Ritual Area, The Offering Wall, and The Spiral Labyrinth. Some of these areas of the land have been used for decades for spiritual purposes. This consistent, constant spiritual use has created its own distinct energy in the land—an energy that we and others can use when needed.

Earth energy also includes the energies of the elements and their counterparts. This means the energies of air, fire, water, and earth. We often add these energies to our spellwork. Herbs, resins, oils, flowers, stones, crystals, and moon water are all a part of earth energies, each with their own corresponding intentions. This also includes frequencies and sound waves—the simple act of chanting sends energy outward as sound waves.

The third type of energy we work with is the energy of our deities, angels, and spirit guides. This energy can be known as "divine energy," "ethereal energy," or "spiritual energy." When we call upon a deity in prayer, ritual, or spellwork, we are asking for this type of energy to work with our intention to help it become a reality.

The last type of energy we use is known as "celestial" or "cosmic energy" and incorporates the energies from the sun, moon, and stars. Part of this energy is rolled into your zodiac sign. This is the energy we tap into when we work with the phases of the moon. This type of energy encompasses the different energies from space.

We can combine different types of energies together to push toward our goals. For example, a spell using incense, chants, and dance on a full moon around a bonfire built with woods corresponding to your intention is a good way to cover several energy bases. The more energies we incorporate, the more powerful our working becomes. This isn't to say you must have a huge list of ingredients. Your own energy and your own intention will always be your strongest energy, but the other energies combined do give your workings a boost. For some people, the ceremony of certain spellwork or ritual allows them to enter a state where they can direct and use their energy in a magical manner more efficiently. You need to experiment and see what works best for you. I love to incorporate many different aspects into my spellwork— sometimes. And sometimes I just want something fast, easy, and straight to the point. What works for you one day might not be what you are looking for some other day. That is okay. It is *your* magic. Do it so it works for you.

Because our magical wants and needs do fluctuate, each of the other sections in this book will have a variety of different ways to tackle the same type of problem. This way, you can use what you need, when you need it. A ritualized spellworking can be backed up with daily affirmations and journal writings. Or a journal writing may lead you to start a daily affirmation to build up to a ritualized spellworking. We learn differently. We act differently. We perform our magic differently. I simply cannot emphasize enough the importance of doing what works for you. Within reason, of course.

## Recognize Your Power

Your energy gives you the power to change your environment. To achieve your full power, you must first recognize your own energy. This can be far more difficult than what people realize because we are so often detached from ourselves. To work magic successfully, you must learn to use your own energy and power. The first step in learning to use them is to learn how to recognize them.

Let's start with these easy experiments to see what I mean.

Begin by visualizing yourself when you are hurt. What body language do you give off? What facial muscles do you use? Where do you hold tension? Picture in your mind what you look like when you have been hurt. See it in your mind's eye. Once you see yourself and how you look, project the image outside of yourself. Fix the same look on your face and project it outward. Tighten the muscles where you would hold the tension. Feel it as if it is there weighing you down. Put yourself into your visualization and feel yourself project that energy outward.

Once you feel yourself enter this state, walk up to people you know and gauge their reactions. Do they pick up on the energy you are sending out? Do they notice you are down? You are giving off this energy to those around you. They should feel it. Some people will respond to your energy by feeling more down themselves. Others may send you a boost of positive energy to not only help you, but to counteract the lower vibration you are sending to protect themselves.

You can then do this experiment again by visualizing yourself as happy and energetic. When you see yourself this way, you allow it to happen. Think of a time when you were extra happy. Visualize that moment. Put yourself in it again and feel the same energy you did then. Carry that energy forward with you to the present and again project it out to those around you. How do they react?

You can easily project emotional energies such as happiness or sadness or even anger. These are energies that we work with frequently without even realizing it. We often receive energies, too, without noticing, which in turn can affect the energies we give off to others.

Pay attention to the energies you see and feel other people sending off. Do they appear to be aware they are giving their energy away? Do they seem to know the status of their energy? Is it a positive, uplifting energy or a negative, downtrodden one?

This exercise shows us how easily we flip the switch on and off while turning the dial throughout the day, every day. Every day we decide what energy we are willing to show and what energy we are willing to receive in our normal interactions. Often, though, we do not pay conscious attention to what we are sending or receiving. This leads to habits, and usually not the best ones at that. We often let in and send out far more negativity than we mean to, as we do not know how to properly block it in the first place, much less ground it or convert it to positivity. This book will help you change that.

Each one of us can walk into a room filled with people and use our energy to either boost the mood or dampen it. This exercise also shows how powerful your energy is without you even trying. If you can change the energy of a room without attempting, think what you can do once you understand how to work with the different energies available to you.

Your next step is to pay attention to your energy shifts by spending time throughout your day checking in with the energy you are sending into your environment. Are you radiating positive or negative energy? If you find yourself sending out negative energy, what can you do to shift it to the positive side? Not quite sure? That is okay, as it is a huge part of what this book is about—adjusting or converting energy from negative to positive. Once you read through the book, you will have several tools at your disposal to help you make this energy shift.

 ## JOURNAL EXERCISE

Keep an energy journal throughout the day for two weeks. Set reminder alarms or notifications for random times each day. When your alarm goes off, check your energy. Where is it at? Learning to pay attention to your energy helps you learn to control your energy. This is important for learning how to use other energies later. Since your own energy is your greatest power, learning to control, focus, and direct it is of the upmost importance when performing magic. Magic simply won't work correctly without the proper energy behind it.

# Flipping the Switch

We are made of energy. We can send it and receive it from others, and we can use it to alter our environment. So how do we do it on purpose?

Let's go back to our example with water in its different stages of matter: solid, liquid, and gas. In that scenario, we applied an outside energy source to the water. That energy source was heat. When a new energy source is applied, change happens.

When we do magic, we are the main energy source. We have the option to use the other types of energy we discussed earlier to back up our work and to add more power to it, but our life energy is the main energy source we use. We are the heat in the water example.

We perform magic by learning to control, focus, and direct our energy into creating a desired change or outcome. We take in energy from around us, convert it to our will, and send it back out into the universe. The backup sources we use contribute their energies according to their associated correspondences.

We convert energy in different ways—mainly through spellwork, ritual, meditation, prayers, and affirmations. Each of these workings has its own benefits and situations it is best suited for, and each requires its own set of skills. When we combine these skills together, we influence energies with our desires and magic happens.

# Skills of the Craft

While there are many important skills to utilize in your Craft, including patience, visualization is one of your most essential skills. When you visualize something happening, particularly with an energy shift, you help to make the shift happen. Visualization helps us learn to control, focus, and direct our energies to create the changes we seek.

Is visualization really that important? Yes! This cannot be emphasized enough. And yet, I understand that visualization can be a huge problem for people, which is why I want to cover this skill first. Let's talk a bit about some of the issues with visualization that people face and discuss different ways of overcoming them.

When someone tells me, "Just imagine," I do. I do because my brain is wired to allow me to. The problem is, not everyone's brain is wired the same, and not everyone has had the same experiences to draw from. So, someone tells me to imagine a mountain, and I can suddenly find myself in the Grand Tetons staring out over Jenny Lake. I can smell the fresh air and the pine trees on the breeze. I can hear the cranes calling along with the chipmunk rustling in the leaves. I have also been to the Grand Tetons, where I was able to stare out over Jenny Lake, smell the air, and hear the cranes. This makes visualizing it easy for me. I can quickly and easily put myself back into a place I have been before.

For some people, being told to imagine a mountain sends their brain into overdrive. It doesn't bring up just one mountain. It brings up dozens of different images: the Rocky Mountains, the Smokies, the Alps, Mount Everest, Superstition Mountain, and many more. Then the brain wants to decide which mountain works the best and begins an argument with itself as it goes through pros and cons of each one.

Other people do not have much experience with mountains and therefore have a hard time drawing on any inspiration to base their imagined mountain on. They can't fully visualize it because they do not have the required information to draw upon.

These are issues that can be overcome with prep work before completing your workings. Always read through your spell or meditation first. Remember—the Craft is a practice; we can *practice* all we want. We can practice performing a spell before we perform it for real. We can practice a ritual or meditation before we perform it. Practicing ahead of time allows us to find where issues might exist—needed supplies, pronunciation problems, visualization limitations—and correct them ahead of time. We want our magic to work, and to ensure it does, we need to be able to perform it with confidence. The first few times you try something new, your confidence level may not be the greatest; that's okay. Practice allows us to build our confidence and deal with any roadblocks that may be in the way.

If you come across something you don't know how to pronounce or you aren't sure how to visualize a concept, remember, research is your friend. Google can tell you how to pronounce things with a search asking for the pronunciation. When you aren't sure how to visualize something, you can also do searches for images and videos. A little bit of research can help your visualizations and workings in a big way.

When you feel your visualization may not be the strongest, there is another way to give your working a boost and that is by using your own symbolism. If there are times when you simply cannot visualize something, don't try to visualize it so specifically. Give it a more generic symbolism. For example, often with physical healing work, or any work that takes place inside the body, it might not be the best to visualize the exact process even if you can. Most people do not have the necessary medical knowledge to fully visualize what the inside of the body truly looks like, and some people may find even attempting to visual their insides disturbing. Nothing wrong with that; it's your own personal preference, which needs to be respected.

There are many ways you can use abstract symbolism to help you in these visualizations. For example, bones do not have to be seen as real bone with muscle attached; they can be seen as made of steel or titanium with a robotic appeal. They can be seen as glass with a fragile quality that needs to be strengthened; perhaps the glass bones are visualized as being dipped into vibranium and hardened. What you picture in your mind is important, but it is even more important you understand what it means to you. The emphasis is on what it stands for.

These types of visualizations are also important for energy work, as most people don't physically see the energy they are working with. Not with their eyes. You can visualize it in your mind's eye however works for you. Many people use a colored light to represent energy, with different colors to represent different types of energy.

What matters the most when you are using an abstract type of visualization is another extremely important skill of the Craft—your intention.

Intention is why you are doing a working. Focusing your intention with as many details as possible builds not only the strength of your intention but also your confidence in your working. Your working is nothing without your intention.

Combine intention with visualization, add in energy and some patience, and you have the basic ingredients for all sorts of wonderful magical workings. These are the basics of the Craft, and throughout the rest of this book we will talk about ways of using and combining them to create the future and world you want to live in.

## Self-Sabotage

No amount of magical work will change anything for the better if the work you do in the mundane world is counterproductive. This is a simple cold, hard truth. We cannot do magical work and then sabotage it with what we do in the mundane world and expect our magical work to be the victor. It doesn't work that way. Our magical work must always be backed up with supportive work in the mundane world.

Whenever you do magical workings, think about how you will back it up with your nonmagical workings. Wanting to be a happier person with a bright future is wonderful, but it can be a lot easier to say than to achieve.

We all have traumas, and to become our best, most complete, happiest self, we must deal with those traumas. We will discuss this more in the chapter on shadow work. For now, remember trauma responses can cause us to self-sabotage without realizing it. The more we heal trauma, the more effective our mundane workings are in backing up our magical workings. We must pay close attention to the actions we take in the mundane world to ensure they are supportive of our magic.

If you want a life that is more positive, you must be willing to make the changes required to bring the positivity in and keep the negativity out. Making small changes, one at a time, is easier to work into a routine than trying to do too much at once. As you successfully make changes, your self-esteem and confidence grow. Trying to make large changes all at once may be setting the bar too high. This results in self-sabotage by setting yourself up for failure. Give yourself the advantage of achieving successes by giving yourself more, smaller goals, instead of fewer, larger ones.

When things are tough, break it down into smaller, more manageable parts. Instead of worrying about the month ahead, focus on the week ahead, or the day ahead, or the hour ahead. Being mindful of your present helps create success.

## Ethics and Responsibilities

I am not here to tell you which ethics system to subscribe to. What I will tell you is that most do have certain aspects in common—most importantly, the concept of treating others how you yourself would like to be treated.

Some pathways promise a punishment to what you send out, others do not. Some say your punishment will be worse than what you send out. Some say your punishment will come in your next life. Some consider it consequences, and the idea of punishment is unheard of.

Whatever path you walk, whether it is structured or your own personal eclectic mix, you will have your own set of ethics and responsibilities you subscribe to.

Whatever you believe, remember, it is your *belief.* It is what you have chosen to affirm as your truth. Know what it is you are willing to stand by. Responsibilities are often overlooked while rights are celebrated. Do not forget about the responsibilities of your path, no matter what your path is. Following the ethical and responsibility guidelines of your individual pathway is part of where your spiritual power comes from. Think about it: if you say you believe in something but don't walk the walk, your credibility goes down.

When your credibility goes down, so does your power. I am not referring to your credibility with others; this is your credibility within yourself. You know when you are not living up to your own ideals, and when you aren't, you feel it. It weighs you down. Evaluate your ethics and responsibilities. Write them down in your own Book of Shadows or journal.

Stand by what you believe. Live it. But also remember your beliefs are never set in stone and can be replaced with new ones. The more we learn, the more our beliefs change. This is enlightenment.

Now that we have a basis for starting your workings, let's move on to learning how to incorporate magic into your daily life for a brighter, better future.

 **JOURNAL EXERCISE**

Throughout your workings, keep track of what you do, how you do it, and what outcome you receive. Write down pertinent information in your journal. If you choose to, you may move or copy things into your Book of Shadows later.

# 2
## Everyday Morning Magic

Some days you are probably excited to get out of bed and start the day. Other days, maybe not so much. Lying in bed when you first awaken in the morning is a great place to start your magical workings. If you are someone who likes to hit the snooze button, you can fit in workings between alarms. If you don't already use a snooze on your alarm, you may want to start if you want to ensure you don't fall back asleep and to set time limits on these early morning workings.

Getting out of bed can sometimes feel like one of the most difficult things to do, particularly when depression has a hand in guiding your actions. The good news is, often once we do get moving, it gets easier to move. This is true from both emotional and physical standpoints. Habits kick in once we start moving. Some days you may feel like you are on autopilot. That's okay. We can work with that. For people who have a hard time physically getting out of bed due to medical issues, often the limitations become less with movement—not in all cases, but in some. The key is to get moving. Beginning your magical work while still in bed gives you the opportunity to start your day off on an extra-positive note.

## Say Hello to the Day

How do you normally start your day? Does an alarm blare to wake you from your slumber? While of course I comprehend the reasoning behind obnoxious, loud sounds to pull us from our sleep, is there a better way to wake up?

I can remember the days I used to wake up reaching my arm out to feel for the alarm clock and hit the snooze button, often missing so it would take several tries. I am not what one would call a morning person. With today's technology, I can simply tell my alarm to stop or snooze. I can also use that same technology to help me start my day off on the right foot by not using an alarm that resembles what I would hear if the house were on fire. Think about it—is a sound that is jarring and sets you on edge the best way to start your day? Probably not if you are looking to have more positive experiences in your life.

Whether you use a phone or other device for an alarm, you can choose from all kinds of different sounds to wake up with. Some devices will allow you to set up an entire morning routine when your alarm goes off. In this way, you can allow an AI assistant to walk you through a morning routine.

Even without an AI interface to assist, you can create a morning routine to follow each day. Let's look at examples of both types of morning routines and then we can get into some specifics on setting up your own.

My morning alarm on my Alexa device plays chimes at an increasing volume. It doesn't jerk me awake; it lets me wake up more slowly and gradually, allowing for a few moments in the between-world of the waking and the sleeping. When I say good morning, I can be given a morning affirmation, followed by a meditative song in which I can work with the affirmation. I can take in a quick meditation and finish up with my daily horoscope and weather report. All before opening my eyes if I so wish. Some people may find this idea absolutely atrocious, but for me, it is a much gentler way of waking up than the startling clang of an alarm.

Without the assistance of an AI interface, you may still be able to try different types of alarms to wake you, whether you use a device for an alarm or an alarm clock. There are some clocks available on the market that have much gentler "alarm" sounds than the standard. It's amazing how something as simple as the sound of what you wake up to can make a difference in your day. At the same time, it also makes perfect sense to not start the morning off by scaring yourself awake. You can choose an uplifting song to use as an alarm. Music is a powerful tool for setting a mood. We will use it often in this book.

Once you wake, you can perform one of the following morning meditations, repeat an affirmation, or both before you get out of bed. You obviously won't be doing a full spell or ritual before getting out of bed each day, but there are activities you can do to help start your day off on a positive note as soon as you wake.

 ## JOURNAL EXERCISE

Pay attention to your regular morning routine. How do you wake up each day? How do you feel immediately upon waking? Document your morning activities and feelings for a few days in a row. Next, add in some of the changes to your morning routine. If you change your alarm sound, what do you change it to? If you are someone who has a difficult time adjusting to change, only make one change at a time and give it a few days before adding in another. For example, begin by changing your alarm. After several days, add in a morning affirmation. After several more days, add in a morning meditation. Document the changes you make and reflect on how they change your outlook for the day.

# Affirmation of the Day

Read through this list of affirmations and pick which you want to use. You can write them down on index cards and keep them next to your bed. A small dry-erase board on a nightstand can also be set up the previous night with the next morning's affirmation. What do you want to focus on? What do you need to focus on?

## HEALING EMOTIONAL TRAUMA

* Each new day is a new beginning. Today is a new beginning.
* My life is under my control.
* I make the most of each day given to me. I am blessed.
* I am strong. I am loved. I am at peace.
* I invite health, wealth, and happiness into my life.
* I use boundaries when and where necessary.
* I release that which does not serve me.
* I am healing. I am strong. I am loved.
* I bring strength, curiosity, and hope into each day.
* I welcome peace and kindness into my life.

## BUILDING CONFIDENCE

* I accept myself for who I am. I am right where I should be.

* Today is the first day of the rest of my life. Each day is a new beginning, a new start.

* I claim this day as my own. It is mine to make the most of.

* I am brave. I am strong. I am fearless.

* I am the best me I can be.

* Today my light will shine.

* Today I will be confident and joyful.

* I make room for new opportunities.

* I am free to be me.

* I am all that I am meant to be.

## SHIFT YOUR PERSPECTIVE

* I rise with the sun. Bright and ready for my day.

* I look forward to what the day may bring.

* As I breathe in, as I breathe out, I prepare for the day ahead.

* I am confident in myself and ready for what the day will bring.

* I am ready for any challenge set before me today.

* As I awaken for the day, I awaken my mind to new experiences.
* I let go of my sleep and prepare for a new day of learning and loving.
* I start my day with an open heart and an open mind.
* I welcome abundance into my life. I welcome in joy.
* Today I will spread the joy of me.

## ENCOURAGING SELF-LOVE

* I stand on the side of love. Love for myself, love for others.
* Today I will care for me. Today I will do my best for me.
* I welcome each new day I am given.
* I am happy with myself. I am the perfect me.
* I am blessed. I am whole. I am complete.
* I accept myself for who I am. I love myself for who I am.
* I live to love—myself, others, the world.
* I was made to be me. I am who I am.
* I live my truth, today and every day.
* I trust myself. I have faith in who I am.

## ENLIGHTENMENT, CHOOSING A SPIRITUAL LIFE

* I choose the path before me. My steps are my own.
* As I open my eyes, I open my mind to a new day.
* Today I welcome love and joy into my life.
* Today I embrace happiness and love.
* I am positive. I am peace. I am love.
* I honor love and life.
* I am a part of the whole. The universe is not complete without me.
* I walk my path with grace, through all twists and turns.
* I honor the light within me.
* I am filled with love—love for myself and love for others.

Affirmations are the perfect way to set an intention for the day.

# Morning Meditations

Starting off with a quick morning meditation gives you the chance to fully set the tone and intention for your day. Giving yourself the few minutes it takes for a brief meditation is in itself an act of self-love. In this section, you will find several brief meditations you can do before leaving your bed. You can do these on your own or in combination with an affirmation. If you can, add some cheery, uplifting music without having to leave your bed. Plan on what meditation you would like to do the night before and read through it several times to get yourself familiar with it. Leave yourself a note next to the bed or a digital reminder to help you perform the meditation in the morning until you are more proficient at them.

Using a snooze feature lets you perform a morning meditation before leaving bed without having to worry about falling back to sleep, and of course this gives you the opportunity to set the snooze for the amount of time you want. Five to ten minutes for one of these meditations is plenty of time.

## GENTLE WAKE-UP MEDITATION

We have been programmed to believe jumping out of bed, slapping off the alarm, and barreling full steam ahead is the only ideal way to wake up each day. There is no one-size-fits-all in anything, including how we wake and start our day. It's not a race. You can take as much time as you need to get yourself ready for the day, and that includes spending a few moments to allow yourself to wake from your slumber in a more gentle, peaceful way.

After you wake, close your eyes again and allow yourself to slip into the time in between sleeping and waking. We often call this "resting our eyes." The intention isn't to fall asleep, but it isn't to be overly conscious either. This in-between time has its own magic. It is as if we are in both places at once, and yet in neither. Take the opportunity to not only notice this special time but allow yourself to become at one with it. It may feel like a waking dream to you. Allow yourself to be only in the present moment—neither totally awake nor asleep.

When you are ready, slowly begin to become aware of your surroundings. If you are using a snooze alarm, nature sounds, windchimes, or another simple and serene sound is a perfect way to announce it is time to become aware of your surroundings. Consciously, yet gently, pull or shift yourself from the in-between space to the waking world. No need for a blaring alarm screaming at you to get out of bed. A gentle, easy shift allows you to start your day without a startling experience. No anxiety from the sudden change from sleep to awake. No panic at a loud, sudden sound. Just a gentle shift from one magical existence to another—though the second is a bit more concrete.

Taking these few extra moments to acknowledge and experience the magic of the in-between sleep and waking time also helps teach us how to recognize other moments when magic shifts us to an in-between space or time.

## BODY SCAN MEDITATION

This meditation is particularly good for people who suffer from any type of chronic pain no matter what the source of the pain is. In this meditation, you will focus on only the physical aspects of your body: a scan to see how everything is feeling and to give you a heads-up as to what you may be dealing with before you start to move around. A body that is moved when it isn't ready can suffer unexpected sprains, strains, or cramps. Getting up too quickly without being sure your body is ready for movement can also cause vertigo, dizziness, or falls. A quick meditative check-in can help avoid mishaps.

With your eyes closed, begin with your toes. Slowly wiggle them back and forth. Curl them tightly, hold for a few seconds, and release. Flex your feet, rotate your ankles, tighten your calves, and let them all relax. Is everything okay so far? If you come across anything that hurts, any areas that are tender, achy, or tense, make a mental note on where you need some extra care. Don't make any judgments about the pain, only note it is there and that it may need special attention later. Bend your knees, leaving your feet flat on the bed. Let your knees fall to the side, first to the left, then to the right. Allow your feet to slide back down the bed, straightening your legs into a comfortable position.

Focus on your abdomen. Tighten and release your core muscles, inspecting the results as you continue to travel upward through your body. Make your hands into tight fists, relax, stretch your fingers apart as far as you can, and relax again. Raise your shoulders toward your ears, relax. Rotate your head left then right, relax. Bend your arms, folding them around you for a gentle hug. Hold yourself for a moment as you tighten and release your facial muscles.

Make note of any place you need to be careful with or any pains you need to attend to once you are ready to get out of bed. Take a few deep, calming breaths, release your self-hug, and open your eyes.

## BRIGHT NEW DAY MEDITATION

As I have gotten older, my views on summer days have completely changed from when I was a child. Back then, I couldn't stand the sunlight shining into my bedroom window because it would wake me up so early. Now, however, I have a much deeper appreciation for the sunlight that streams through my windows. With the way my house is situated, I often don't close my eastern bedroom curtains, so the sun comes in as soon as it begins breaking through the trees. What used to be aggravating to me is now instead inviting. The sun coming through my window is often my favorite part of the morning, particularly when accompanied by cat snuggles.

This meditation is to help you capture the energy of the sunrise and hold it in your power throughout the day.

Before you open your eyes, begin your meditation by recalling an image of just before dawn. The sun has not yet broken the horizon, but the colors of twilight are glowing. You know that the sunrise you are about to see will be spectacular. Perhaps the sunrise you expect to see may be a moment you have previously experienced that you found to be profound or meaningful and would like to relive. If you haven't personally seen a sunrise that strongly spoke to you, that is okay. Is here an image you have seen in a movie, on TV, in a photograph, in a painting, or from somewhere else you can draw to mind of a particularly brilliant, bright sunrise?

Focus on the moment right before the sun breaks the horizon line. The color of the sky around you changes. It begins to lighten, a little more, a little more, and then the first rays break over the horizon. Focus on the colors you see. Feel the rays of the sun as they reach out to warm your skin. Follow the sunrise in your mind for several minutes, allowing it to rise to the ideal picture for you. Soak in the heat, the energy, the power of the sun. Feel the light as it reaches and blends with your energetic field. Visualize the light charging you like a solar battery. Take in as much light and energy as you can, storing it throughout all of you. Fill yourself with as much of the light as you can. Let it wash over you, warm you, and charge you.

Hold on to this feeling for a few moments in silence. You can store this light, this energy, and carry it with you for the rest of the day. When you are ready, open your eyes.

If you need a pick-me-up during the day, simply close your eyes for a moment, recall the image and feeling, then allow that burst of energy to release and give yourself a boost.

## SLAY THE DAY MEDITATION

Some days, you know you are going to have a tough day ahead of you, which can make getting out of bed a bit more difficult. This meditation is for those days. Empower and prepare yourself before ever leaving your bed by ensuring you see yourself as conquering whatever obstacles may stand in your way.

If necessary, set your snooze, timer, or other alarm. If you would like to play music along with this meditation, be sure to have it prepared ahead of time.

With your eyes closed, take a few deep breaths. Instead of focusing on what obstacles you must deal with today, set those aside and focus on seeing yourself in a strong, positive image. You may choose whatever image of strength you want to emulate. You can be a superhero, a knight in shining armor, a powerful witch or wizard, a Transformer, a god. Think indestructible. Unbeatable. You can channel the energy of whatever you want. You can be whatever, whomever you want. It is your choice. Take on the added strength from your visualization. How can you incorporate this strength into helping you today? How can it help you overcome and complete the challenges that lie in front of you? Remember, you can visualize your challenges with symbolism instead of a more literal visualization. Do what works for you and allows you to see yourself slaying any obstacle in your way.

Have fun with this meditation. Be creative and let your imagination run wild. Today, nothing can stop you. You are full of confidence. The day is yours. You are a powerhouse. Pump yourself up, build the energy in your mind. Focus it on slaying the day and begin directing your energy when you are ready by opening your eyes.

# Theme Songs and the Soundtrack of Life

Music is a powerful tool. The sound of it can instantly bring back memories; it can transport you to a different time and place. It can help you sleep and help you wake up. It is as ideal with gentle meditation as it is with active exercise. It can help you feel empowered. It can boost your confidence. It can raise your spirits. It can help to mend a broken heart.

Do you have a theme song for your life? Music lovers will often already have one (or several) picked out. Your theme song is a song that can either touch or represent you deeply. You feel you could have written it yourself. It speaks to you on a more personal level than most other music. Theme songs may change over time, or you may add new titles to your theme song collection; you may have many theme songs on your soundtrack of life. As life goes on and you grow and evolve, you might set an entire soundtrack aside and conduct a new symphony to take its place.

Using theme songs and playlists is an easy way to add the energy from sound waves to your workings, and to give even mundane tasks a hint of magic. Music contains the energy put into its making. It also triggers an energy response in the listener. These energies combine, allowing them to grow and become stronger. The energy from music can feed the energy of your personal life force. Adding music to your workings, no matter what type it is, allows you to build more energy.

As a part of the getting-older generation, I can attest to how much easier it is to have music accompany your life these days than it ever has been before. The digital age and streaming services not only make music instantly and conveniently available, but they are also responsible for giving musicians a broader market and for connecting listeners to a much larger array of talent. With music as accessible as it now is, it would be a shame not to tap into this energy source and use it for your benefit.

Spend time exploring music and creating playlists to help you in your magical workings. There are many different types of playlists you may want to have in your library. Topic titles include:

* Morning Meditations
* Morning Routines
* Sleep Meditations
* Bedtime Routines
* Empowerment Songs
* Energy Raising Songs
* Chill Lounge for Relaxing
* Workout Playlist
* Songs to Make Me Smile

There are others you can make, but these are the basics for your musical treasury. Make whatever other lists you feel the need to make. Using music in your practices is like lighting a candle, in the sense that both the music and candle are tools you can use to help achieve your overall goal. Instead of storing this set of tools in a wooden chest or placing them on an altar, you store them on a device or in the cloud.

I often listen to other people's playlists or streaming stations while I am working as background music, then when a new song I like comes on, I can easily add it to the appropriate playlist or lists. I love how easy it is to incorporate music into every aspect of my day with the technology we now have available.

Many music services offer the "if you like this, then you may like this" feature. Use it! This is another great way to discover new music that speaks to you.

Remember, literally anything you do can be made more magical, more powerful, more intense, more energetic, more somber, more of whatever you want it to be, by adding music to it.

## Stretch and Be Active

Studies have shown that being active helps to put people into a happier, more positive mood.[1] The problem is, it's also easier to be active when you are already in a happier, more positive mood. You must make the first step to get the ball rolling; once

---

1. Felipe B. Schuch, Davy Vancampfort, Joseph Firth, et al., "Physical Activity and Incident Depression: A Meta-Analysis of Prospective Cohort Studies," *American Journal of Psychiatry* 175, no. 7 (July 2018): 631–648, https://doi.org/10.1176/appi.ajp.2018.17111194.

you start moving, you start producing more endorphins, which make you feel better and make you feel like being more active.

Begin your day with simple stretches. Take the time to really check in with your body by focusing on the muscles in use with each stretch you perform. Begin while in bed if you like, working your way into a sitting position, and then finally into standing.

If you have chronic pain, stretching allows your body to start activating and gives you a heads-up on where issues may be lurking. Not only do you know what part of your body to be more cautious with, you have locations to start sending healing energy. Those without chronic pain still benefit from the slow stretching approach to getting out of bed since it is another way to practice the mind and body connection.

If you are not used to being active, there are easy ways to begin that are less strenuous but allow you to build intensity into your practice as you are ready to level up. Yoga and walking are both low-impact and low-intensity ways to add in activity. As you progress, your skills, stamina, and strength will too. Build yourself up to a minimum of twenty minutes of activity a day. If it's easier to do it all at once, great! If not, you can break it up throughout the day.

Being physically active and allowing your body to produce endorphins is an important way to back up your magical workings with your mundane workings. The more you move, the more endorphins you produce, the happier your body can keep you. Your body is designed to make you feel good and give you pleasure. Using the biological tools your body has to improve positive feelings is the most natural type of magic there is.

Activity and exercise also build energy you can use magically. Use this energy to send intentions into the universe. Adding affirmations while building energy, such as with dance or drumming, is an excellent way to quickly boost positivity. Combining magical and mundane tasks together is key to being successful in creating a brighter future. They go together hand in hand.

Mornings set the tone for the day. Work to create a routine that leaves you feeling refreshed, invigorated, and ready for whatever adventures lie ahead.

 ### Journal Exercise

Analyze your current morning routine and find the things you do out of habit that may not have a beneficial result. Replacing habits helps us achieve our goals. What is something you do now that you can replace with exercise? For many, it's time watching TV. If you like to watch the news in the morning, do some exercises along with it.

Record how you feel both before and after your workout. Can you feel the increase in endorphins as they boost your mood?

# 3
## Water Works

Showering and bathing are acts of cleansing not only physically but emotionally, mentally, and, if you wish, spiritually. This makes the shower or bathtub a great place for morning spellwork that is designed to wash away any negativity and boost your mood and energy level. In this section, you will learn different ways to refresh and recharge yourself with easy spellwork to perform in your shower or tub.

Prepare your ingredients ahead of time so they are all ready to go when you need them. Running around trying to pull ingredients together in the morning may interrupt your energetic flow or cause issues if you are already crunched for time. Do as much of the preparation for your morning workings as you can the night before. You can make these preparations a part of your nighttime routine. Some preparations—like shower steamers—take more time, so always be sure to plan ahead when you can.

# Morning Revitalizer

This working is for those of you who don't mind mornings but still have an issue with grogginess when you wake. Morning brain fog can easily be lifted with this citrusy recipe for a shower steamer. To use a shower steamer, you place it on the floor of your shower and the water activates the baking soda to release the scent of the essential oils. To make it last longer, place it on the opposite side of the shower from your drain so the water hits it, but it isn't standing in water.

Shower steamers are like bath bombs, the main difference being the amount of moisture used when making them. Shower steamers are drier and therefore denser, making them take a longer time to dissolve in water, but they can still be used in the tub.

For this recipe you will need:

* A mold for your steamers—generally these are a square shape about an inch thick, but you can choose any design you wish.
* ½ cup baking soda
* ¼ cup citric acid
* A spray bottle filled with witch hazel
* 7 drops lemon essential oil

* 7 drops orange essential oil
* 7 drops tangerine essential oil
* Plastic gloves

Wearing plastic gloves, blend together the baking soda and citric acid, ensuring it is mixed well. Next add the drops of essential oils, spreading them out as much as you can over the dry ingredients. Blend extremely well, being sure to break up any clumps. Mist the mixture with five sprays of the witch hazel and blend together again. When you are able to press the mixture into a shape and it stays, it is ready. If it does not stick yet, continue adding two sprays at a time and mixing again until you reach the desired consistency. Pack the mixture into your mold and allow to sit overnight. Remove the steamer from your mold and either use it or store in airtight container.

As you prepare this steamer, instill it with your energy. It contains several different kinds of energy already from the ingredients, but you can add your energy as an additional ingredient. Visualize, in a way that works for you, your energy charging the mixture with joy and happiness. You can add more energy to the process of making the steamer by adding music while you work. A couple of lit yellow and orange candles in your workspace help to instill your working with joy and energy.

While you blend your ingredients together, use this chant to help build, focus, and direct your energy into what you are doing:

*This song I sing*
*To my work will bring*
*Magic from my soul.*
*Energy raised*
*Focus sent*
*Mixing in this bowl.*

When you are ready to use the steamer, place it on the floor of your shower. If you are taking a bath, pop it in the tub. As the water hits it and releases the scent into the air, close your eyes, take several deep breaths, and allow the scent and water both to wash over you. Visualize the citrusy scent scrubbing away at your gray grogginess with bright yellow and orange energy.

As you visualize this happening, reach out to the deity of your choice or the universe and say:

*Please help to take away that which clutters my*
*mind, wash away what interferes with my ability*
*to be at my best.*

*Bless me in your peace and light as I look to you*
*for guidance on my path.*

Let it scrub away the brain fog, which is then washed away down the drain.

# Refresh and Recharge

This working is for those who have a physically difficult time getting moving in the morning. If you suffer from chronic pain or inflammation, this one is directed toward you, and you will need a trip to the produce section of the grocery store, a farm stand, or your own herb garden for a bunch of fresh peppermint and rosemary.

To make this type of working easy in the future, you do need to do some prep work in your shower, but once it is done, you will be able to use it over and over for this and other workings. Place a plant hook in your shower ceiling so that when you hang your herbs from it, they will be hit by the water close to the showerhead. Tie a ribbon or string to the hook, and on the other end attach a spring-activated clothespin. Make the ribbon or string long enough so that you can reach it and yet pin it up out of the way with the clothespin when it is not in use.

Prepare the herbs the day before by tying a string around the stems of the peppermint and rosemary, bundling them together. If you happen to have a yellow or orange ribbon you can use, all the better to add in a little bit more focus and boost the energy. As you wrap the string or ribbon around the stems to bind them together, focus on your intent. When you use this bundle, you want to feel refreshed and recharged and ready for the day. You want pain to subside. You want positivity. Think about those things now and pour that intent into

47

the string as you wrap it and tie it around the stems. Store this in the refrigerator until you are ready to use it.

When you are ready to shower, throw on a playlist that makes you feel energized. Take the bound peppermint and rosemary bundle and use the clothespin to snap it in place in front of the shower head before turning on the water. Scrunch the fresh leaves in your hands a few times and appreciate the feel of the coolness against your skin. As you scrunch the leaves, you release their essences and energies. Turn the water on and allow the water to pass over the leaves and to you, carrying the energies with it.

If you prefer to use a bath, prepare the herbs as mentioned. Scrunch the leaves under the running faucet as the tub fills. When you have your desired water level, use the herb bundle to stir the water in a clockwise motion. Remember to send a healing intent into the water through your herb bundle.

Close your eyes and take several deep breaths, allowing the scent to fill your head and lungs. Take in its healing properties. Take in its power to refresh you, allowing you to feel reenergized. Keep the herb bundle in place throughout your shower, or let it float in the tub with you. When you are finished, use the bundle to gently shake off the excess water over yourself. If you can, allow yourself to air dry naturally. You can reclip the peppermint and rosemary with the clothespin to allow it to dry out and to leave your bathroom smelling fresh.

# Spiritual Cleansing

Remember, maintaining spiritual health is as important as maintaining your physical and emotional health, which means spiritual cleansing is as important as physical and emotional cleansing. You may feel you need spiritual cleansing for different reasons. While a nightmare may leave you feeling spiritually vulnerable, you also may feel the need for spiritual cleansing due to the ingrained trigger of guilt. Whatever your reasons, they are your reasons and between you and your higher power or higher self. Because we need to take our spiritual health seriously, this working will be a ritual style, which helps convey its importance.

For this working you will need:

* A white candle in a firesafe container in a safe place in or near the shower or tub

* A second firesafe container with a handle—this one should have either sand or salt in the bottom and a self-lighting charcoal tablet on top of the sand/salt. Ensure the bottom will not get too hot and scorch whatever it is set upon. This, too, should have a safe place to sit in or near the shower or tub. A small cast iron cauldron would be perfect.

* A lighter

* A mix of frankincense and myrrh resins—as little or as much as you like. You can always start small and add more if you want to.

When you are undressed and ready, light the white candle and call to your deity, the universe, or your higher self by saying:

*I call upon [insert name or title]*
*As I perform this sacred consecration.*
*Be with me now to guide me on my path.*

Light the charcoal tablet in the firesafe container. (An open window is a good idea.)

Once it is ready (has turned red or ashen), add a few pieces of the frankincense and myrrh resins to the charcoal tablet. They will start smoking immediately. Using the handle, move your cauldron or container all around the shower area, filling it as much as you can with the smoke and then placing it in a safe spot. Keeping the door or curtain closed will allow you to keep more smoke in the area, but be sure not to make it too smokey as to cause any breathing issues. Do not yet turn the water on, but instead, begin bathing yourself in the smoke. As you bathe in the smoke, say slowly (take your time as you allow the smoke to drift around you) either to yourself or aloud:

*I stand in sacred smoke,*
*Naked before the universe,*

*My spirit and soul to be cleansed.*
*I stand in sacred smoke,*
*Naked with the universe,*
*My spirit and soul at one with all.*
*I stand in sacred smoke,*
*Naked before the universe,*
*My spirt and soul cleansed.*

When you are ready, turn on the water and visualize your spirit being rinsed clean as the smoke disperses. Finish by showering or bathing as normal.

## Healing Waters

While this isn't guaranteed to heal all that ails you, it will help clear stuffy sinuses, congested lungs, a scratchy throat, and possibly a headache. These types of symptoms aren't what you want to deal with starting off your day, so if you feel an illness coming on, be sure to pick up a bunch of fresh eucalyptus to keep on hand.

Tie up the eucalyptus with twine to hang on the hook with the clip in your shower or place it so the water from the tub faucet will run over it. You can leave fresh eucalyptus in your shower for about three weeks, which should be plenty of time to clear your head or chest.

Eucalyptus has incredible healing energies, but we won't leave it up to just the plant. To prepare for this working, find a safe place for some green candles. (If there is no place in your shower or tub where you can safely use candles, don't forget the tank on the toilet. This is often a place where you can set up some candles in safety containers. Don't use taper, chimes, or spell-size candles. Instead use jars, tins, or full votive holders.) Add some waterfall music on a nearby device, and you are ready to begin.

Before entering the shower or tub, ensure the eucalyptus is hanging where it will get wet. Allow the shower to run as hot as it can for a few minutes to build up steam and release the scent from the eucalyptus. Be sure to turn the water cooler again before getting in! Inhale deeply through your nose several times while exhaling through your mouth. Switch your breathing pattern by inhaling through your mouth a couple of times while exhaling through your nose. This is a little bit more difficult to do, so be aware of the possibility of light-headedness. Return your breathing to normal.

See yourself feeling better, breathing easily, all signs of malaise are gone. Focus on this image as you breathe in and out, inhaling the healing scent and energies of the eucalyptus.

Finish your shower or bath as normal. After you get out, again turn the water as hot as you can to steam up the air with the eucalyptus one more time to get one last boost.

For morning work, before you leave the shower or tub, for the last few seconds turn the water cold for an invigorating splash.

While a shower or bath will not cure everything, it does give you the space and time for a reset to help keep you on the right path. One step at a time gets you where you need to be.

# Bath Workings

Taking a bath at night is not only a great way to wind down at the end of the day, but also a great way to add in more water magic to your routine. These workings include bath salts, a meditation, and an affirmation.

## WASH AWAY THE DAY BATH SALTS

These bath salts will help you release what ails you after a long or tough day. While you are combining ingredients and blending them together, send peaceful, relaxing energy into what you are working with. Visualize something you find to be peaceful or use your energy color representation and send peaceful energy into your working. What can you add to your workings to make it stronger? You can light candles in corresponding colors. Working with relaxing music will help you to boost this energy.

For these bath salts you will need:

* 1 cup of any combination of bath salts: Epsom salts, sea salt, pink Himalayan salt

* 2 tablespoons lavender

* 2 tablespoons chamomile

* A bowl and spoon or spatula for mixing

* Any 8 ounce jar with a lid

* Optional: colloidal oatmeal for baths

Combine all the ingredients in a bowl and mix until well combined, then transfer into a jar that has an airtight lid. Depending on how much you choose to use, this mixture should last 4–8 baths.

## WASH AWAY THE DAY MEDITATION

Using the bath salts above, prepare your bath with comfortably warm water. Add relaxing candles where (and if) it is safe to do so. For your audio pleasure, do a search for "waterfall music." This will give you plenty of options that include relaxing music with the natural sounds of waterfalls and moving water.

If you are comfortable with it, turn out the lights and use candlelight only. (If you cannot do candles safely, look for other dimmer light options such as a plug-in night-light or a tap light.) Submerge yourself into the tub and get comfortable. Allow yourself a few moments to appreciate the warmth of the water. Close your eyes and take several deep breaths, inhaling for a count of five, holding for a count of five, and exhaling for a count of five.

Listen to the music with the sounds of flowing water. Visualize yourself in a serene setting where you can bathe in a private lagoon filled by a waterfall. It doesn't have to be a huge, grand waterfall; a small one, with the strength of a strong shower, is plenty. This area is for you, so make it what you want it to be. Add in any details you like or make it as vague as you like. Visualize it in a way that works for you.

You are here to relax and wash away any stress from the day. This doesn't mean you are forgetting about any problems, only stripping away the stress any problems brought with them. We can learn to deal with our problems without letting stress get to us; we only have to learn how. Problems are seldom solved by stress alone. Once we realize we decide how we are going to react to problems, dealing with problems gets easier. That isn't to say they go away, but we can learn how to handle and solve them while not letting them bring additional fallout along for the ride. Since we don't need stress to solve our problems, we can let it wash away.

Imagine you are washing away all stress or other negativity at the end of the day. Maybe you watch it roll off you as you float in your private lagoon. Maybe you watch it wash off like chunks of mud as you stand underneath the waterfall, water running all over you. Perhaps you visualize stress and negativity as a dingy color that washes from you and swirls away downstream. Use what works for you to see yourself being cleansed of stress and refreshed. When the stress is gone, we can function and sleep better. Being sure not to take stress to bed with you isn't easy. It takes a conscious effort of ridding both your mind and body of it first. Making these conscious efforts to put your own emotional wellbeing first is some self-care at its finest.

## WASH AWAY THE DAY AFFIRMATIONS

Adding in affirmations helps tell yourself what you need. When your body and mind want to hold on to stress, tell them to stop and let go instead. This is part of how affirmations work—repeating something enough makes it come true for you. It's an incredible power that we have, and we need to make sure we are using it properly.

When you have washed the stress away with your meditation, before you leave the tub, use any of the following affirmations to back up your working. You may pull the plug and allow the water to drain away as you finish up.

* My stress is washed away.
* I am in control of my reactions.
* What does not serve me washes away.
* I am cleansed and free from stress and negativity.
* I am refreshed, relaxed, and ready for bed.

## MEDICATE AND MEDITATE HEALING BATH SALTS

Whether the medicine you use in your life is a pharmaceutical, cannabis, CBD, or the act of relaxing in the bath, you know what helps heal you and makes you feel better. This working is all about healing. Use this tub-time working to medicate however you need to and then follow up with the healing meditation and affirmation below.

For these bath salts you will need:

* 1 cup Epsom salts

* ½ tablespoon chamomile

* ½ tablespoon lavender

* ½ tablespoon peppermint

* ½ tablespoon rosemary

* A bowl and spoon or spatula for mixing

* Any 8 ounce jar with an airtight lid

* Optional: colloidal oatmeal for baths

Combine all the ingredients in a bowl and mix until well combined, then transfer into a jar that has a lid. Depending on how much you choose to use, this mixture should only last one to two baths. (You may use it all at once or half a cup at a time.) Epsom salts are beneficial to healing aches and pains, but you do need to soak for at least twenty minutes.

## HEALING MEDITATION

Increase your healing energies by combining your healing bath with a healing meditation.

Adding green and/or blue candles in firesafe containers where you can will also add extra healing energies to your working.

Begin running the water for your bath. Hold the jar of salts in both of your hands and say either out loud or to yourself (directed toward your higher power): *Bless this salt and these herbs with your healing touch.*

Imagine what the energy of the blessing would feel like. Visualize it. Feel it. Honor it.

Slowly scatter the salt in a clockwise motion around your tub. As you scatter the salt, watch how it incorporates with and then dissolves into the water. The energies are combining. The herbs will float on top, the water steeping their essences out to blend with the salted water.

After you have added all the salts, use your hand to gently stir the water three times clockwise. If you have quartz or hematite stones (hematite will eventually rust in water, so do not repeatedly use the same stone), you can hold these in your hand as you stir and then drop them into the tub. Again, you are adding more healing energies with everything you bring to your working. While you stir, visualize all these different energies mixing; see each as a different color swirling together into a portal of healing. Step into this portal and get yourself into a comfortable position. Towels can be rolled to place behind the back or the neck if needed. Once you are comfortable, begin some deep breathing. Inhale and exhale, holding each for a count of four several times, followed by holding for a count of five for several more.

Allow your body to relax. Water allows you to feel lighter; enough of it can make you feel weightless. Focus on this feeling. Allow yourself to float as much as you can, both physically and spiritually. See yourself floating in the healing portal of energies. Visualize the healing energies swirling around you in a clockwise motion, scrubbing pain into the water to later be washed down the drain. These energies regenerate and rejuvenate where needed. Out with the old, dull, painful energy. In with the clean, fresh, pain-free energy.

Remember, Epsom salts need twenty minutes to work optimally, so you need to plan to stay in the tub at least this long. If you need to warm your water up, go ahead. When you are ready to leave the tub, pull the plug and stand while you visualize the pain swirling down the drain. Let it all go.

# Healing Affirmations

Boost your healing energies by adding in affirmations. These can be done before, during, or after your bath, and whenever you feel the need to boost your healing power.

* I work to heal myself.
* Strength surrounds me. It permeates me.
  It makes me healthy and strong.
* I am whole. I am complete.
* My body is strong. My spirit is strong. My body
  and spirit work to heal me.
* I release pain. I release illness. I release all that
  ails me.

Water magic is, by its very nature, cleansing. Remember to focus on washing away whatever negativities you must contend with, while enriching your spirit with positive energies instead.

# 4
## Love, Pray, Eat

F ood is one of our most important sources of energy, and one we must replenish daily to survive.

It is important to understand your relationship with food, evaluate if it is a healthy relationship, and if necessary, adjust where needed. A healthy relationship with food includes not overindulging and knowing and understanding what your food is and where it comes from. This knowledge changes your attitude, allowing you to reach true gratefulness for what you have. It helps you to gain a new perspective and appreciation. Most importantly, your food is your main energy source. Be mindful of what kinds of energies you are consuming.

Knowing what is in your food allows you to make a stronger connection with it. Preparing food yourself is one way to ensure you know precisely what is in it. When you prepare your own food, you can also bless it as you work. Some religions have extremely strict codes dating back centuries for how they prepare and bless food. It is not a new idea, but one that has often been pushed to the side in exchange for convenience.

When preparing your food, you can focus and direct your energy and intention into your preparation as you would with any other working. The ingredients you use can support your intention and will contribute their own energy. The setting in which you create your recipes will also contribute to the energy you infuse into them.

Lighting colored candles, playing music, burning incense, or diffusing oils into the air, even dancing, are all ways to help build, focus, and direct your energy while preparing yourself a meal.

As you recite a blessing, hold your dominant (or power) hand over the food you are working with. Visualize the energy transferring from your hand into your meal. When you are finished with a blessing, you will want some type of closing to tie it all up. Closings include "Amen," "So mote it be," "Blessed be," or even a simple "The end." Use the closing that speaks to you.

Music, incense, and candles during a meal help to set an ambience to emphasize your intention.

## Salt and Pepper Protection Blessing

I love to use a bit of kitchen witchery in my practice, and there are many simple ways to do so. One of the easiest is the act of adding salt and pepper to a meal. Not only do these spices add flavor and a wee bit of pizazz, but they also add protection. Since they both have protective properties, you can focus your intention on infusing a dish with protection for the person who eats the food.

Chant the following as you sprinkle salt and pepper into your recipes:

> *Salt of the earth,*
> *Pepper from the vine,*
> *Let us work together.*
> *Protect what is mine.*

Easy, to the point, and effective.

This should be just the beginning of learning the properties and correspondences of the herbs and spices you use. Having this knowledge gives you more control in what energies you direct into your food preparation.

## Healing-Infused Food Blessing

It doesn't matter what type of food you are preparing; you can use this healing-infused working for anything. Whether it's a gourmet meal or pouring a cup of coffee, all that changes is how long you keep your working going.

To begin this working, I want you to shake your arms and hands in the air for a minute or two first. Really shake them. Feel the energy in them? Visualize the energy you feel as green. Whatever shade of green you want, but be sure it is bright and vibrant. A shade of green that looks rich and healthy to you. Visualize the green energy in your arms and hands. Hold it there as you begin to prepare whatever you are making. In your mind, see the bright, healthy green energy seep from your fingers and into what you are doing.

For example, if you are making a cup of coffee, visualize the green energy transferring from your fingers to the machine, the cup, the spoon, the water, if there is a pod—everything you touch, infuse your healing energy into it. Let it travel a path from you to the final food or drink product you make. Once it reaches its destination, allow the energy to swirl, scatter, and dissipate, being absorbed by what you made.

Working with green candles lit and a healing scent such as eucalyptus, tea tree, lemon, or lavender in the air will help add to the energy you build and infuse into your meal.

## Gratitude Food Blessing

Gratitude is an important aspect of any practice. When we work with manifestations or conduct spellwork, we are asking to receive from the universe. There are many ways to give thanks for the blessings we have received and continue to receive. A great time to practice gratitude is while preparing a meal, like some cultures pray and give thanks before eating.

Gratitude mostly comes from intention, and gratitude workings focus primarily on the flow of energy. There are also tools that can be used to amplify your intentions. A gratitude candle allows you to channel your intentions and is a great tool to enhance this practice. The candle can be any color that you associate with gratitude—green to represent the abundance in your life, pink for compassion and nurturing, light blue for peace and tranquility, purple as connection to a divine power, or white for unity and purity. Herbs associated with success and manifestation are great to use in gratitude workings, such as bay laurel, cinnamon, lemon balm, and basil, also known as holy basil. These herbs can be burned as an incense or used to dress your gratitude candle.

When you are ready to begin your gratitude blessing, clear your mind and set your intentions. Ensure that your space is cleansed and full of positive energies. Close your eyes and imagine a warm, soothing energy filling you from within, moving outward to fill your space and your food preparation items. Raise your hands, palms turned upward, and speak your intentions out loud. Express what you are grateful for using these words or choosing to speak from the heart:

> *I am grateful for the meal that will nourish me.*
> *I am grateful for the love around me.*
> *I am grateful for my abundant life.*
> *I am grateful for all that I receive.*

Release your hands as you release the energy outward and open your eyes. Continue to prepare your meal as normal. Show your thanks by leaving a sample of the dish on your altar or placing some outside as an offering.

# Energizing Food Blessing

This energizing blessing will provide metaphysical fuel to your meal, nurturing not just your body but your spirit as well. The first step is to set your intention and prepare your space. Have your recipe and ingredients geared up in advance and get ready to move your body! Set the mood with uplifting citrus scents by diffusing some essential oils or even just laying out orange slices. Open the blinds to let the sunshine in and light some candles.

The next step is to put on some music—anything that speaks to your soul and gets the blood pumping, whether it is an earthy drum jam, an electric beat, or your favorite hip-hop hit. Choose something that empowers you, makes you feel strong, and allows you to tap into your personal power.

As the music starts, close your eyes. Allow yourself to feel the beat and begin to sway to the sound of the music. As your body begins to move, imagine a bright yellow light building around you, warm and full of power. The light fills you while you dance. Direct this energy toward your ingredients and the kitchen tools that you will be using.

This next part may feel silly, but sound is an excellent tool for raising energy. Clap your hands together. Knock on the cabinet doors, drum on the countertops. Pick up a cooking pan and a spatula and bang them together. Laugh, sing, dance, and allow yourself to have fun with this practice. Fill your space with energy as you begin to follow your recipe.

Once your ingredients have all been added and your meal has been prepared, clap your hands loudly three times and declare:

> *I am energized!*
> *My vibration is high.*
> *Each bite fuels my body and mind.*

Release the energy and serve your meal. Let the music continue to play as you eat. This is great for a social setting; allow yourself to laugh, rejoice, and feel the uplifting energy fuel you.

## Positive Vibes Food Blessing

This is a fun way to add a positive boost to any dish you prepare. You can send positive vibes to yourself or to whoever else will be eating the food by setting up your workspace with yellow and orange candles along with music that makes you feel super groovy happy. If you are working with songs with lyrics, take the lyrics into consideration. For example, "Superstition" by Stevie Wonder is one of my favorite grooves, but the last thing I want to do is insert superstitious energies into my food, especially when serving others! Sound waves are energy waves, so be mindful of what energies you are sending. Keep it upbeat and positive.

Gather your ingredients together on a counter or table. Set the candles in a safe place close by and light them. As you light them, say:

*I call upon the powers which be*
*To infuse my working with positivity.*

Turn on your music, and as you prepare the meal, sing along with the song if there are lyrics. Visualize what positive vibrations look like to you. Maybe you see rainbows stretched out and riding through the air like waves. Perhaps positive vibes look like a giant purple smoke cloud after an awesome bong rip. Whatever you see as positive vibes is what counts. Send the energy you are visualizing into the food you are preparing. Watch as the energy soaks in and is absorbed by what you are making.

# Welcome Morning

Whether you break your fast with a cup of coffee, a bowl of fruit, or a full Irish platter, take a moment before your first bite or sip to welcome the morning. If you can, go outside and face the rising sun. If you cannot go outside, gaze out an eastern window, or if there are none, at least face the east. If you can see the sun, it may be easier to imagine feeling the sunlight on your face as you close your eyes. Even if it is not visible, imagine this feeling, this warmth. The feeling of the start of a new day. Fresh. Ready.

If you are a coffee or tea drinker, holding your cup in your hands in front of your face adds to the warmth sensation. If there is no sun to warm your face, this may help enhance that part of your visualization. Be mindful of hot liquids and don't spill on yourself.

Take a few deep breaths as you enjoy the warmth on your skin and say either out loud or in your own mind:

*Each day is a new beginning,*
*Each beginning a fresh new start.*
*Each day I welcome the morning,*
*Each morning I open my heart.*

Giving yourself these special moments throughout the day to connect fully with the present is another small act of self-care. Performing several small acts of self-care a day makes it easy to build these into good, supportive habits.

## Meal Blessings

The act of blessing food goes back thousands of years and over hundreds of traditions. People the world over have seen the importance of blessing what goes into the body. When we can feel the connection between our body, food, and spirit, the act of blessing food adds a new importance. It becomes more of a necessity. We can bless our meals in different ways, just as we can while preparing them. Remember, your intention is what matters the most. You may use blessings in different ways— where you are giving the blessing upon the food or where you are using it more as a prayer and asking for the blessing from a higher power. Read through the blessings and see how you want to use them and make a few adjustments for them to fit.

## BREAKFAST BLESSING

We often hear breakfast is the most important meal of the day. Your body has been in sleep mode, running on empty and generally hasn't had any fuel added to it for hours. It isn't easy to wake up, start your day, and be energized when your energy supply is wiped out. You can push a car with no gas, but only so far before you physically give out and can't do it anymore. Your body is very much like a car out of gas when you first wake up. Skipping breakfast then ends up being counterproductive in the long run.

Taking the time for breakfast, even if it is a small one, helps set you up for a more positive, energetic, happy day. Your body and mood function better when they are properly fueled.

Use this blessing for your breakfast to start your day off right.

*This food is a blessing upon my body.*
*It restores to me strength.*
*It restores to me energy.*
*It provides sustenance for my survival.*
*This food nourishes my body.*
*It is a blessing upon my body,*
*And I accept with an open and grateful heart.*

How we start our day has a tremendous impact on our emotional wellbeing. Starting it off with positivity gives you a wonderful base from which to build your day.

## LUNCH BLESSING

I will be the first to admit, I do not usually eat on a regular schedule. This is something I have struggled with most of my life. It is difficult for me to remember to eat.

Our bodies need fuel. Starving them of this fuel has long-term side effects, including weight gain! Yes, not giving our bodies enough calories when needed causes our bodies to store more calories in case they are needed later. This lunch blessing also serves as a reminder of what our bodies need. When the body is happy, the mind has less to worry about, and we function more efficiently.

This lunch blessing makes for a happy body and mind.

*Blessings upon this food.*
*Let it remind me food is sacred.*
*My health is sacred.*
*My body is sacred.*
*My mind is sacred.*
*What I take in becomes a part of me.*
*It feeds my health.*
*My body.*
*My mind.*
*Blessings upon this food.*

You can use this blessing before you eat, or if you like, continually repeat it to yourself as you do eat. This makes for a powerful mindful moment you can accomplish while getting your lunch in at the same time, and it's a great break and reset before the rest of your day.

## DINNER BLESSING

While it is often said breakfast is the most important meal of the day, dinner is the one most people consistently eat. It is the last meal (late-night snacks not included). It is a moment to sit down, relax, and refuel. Sometimes, it is a celebration of having made it through the day. Let your dinner become a transition period for you. The hustle and bustle of the day is behind you. Even if you still have things to do, take this time to downshift into a slower gear. Allow your body to work with the natural rhythms of the world and begin the transition of winding down for the night. This is especially important for those who have a difficult time shutting down their mind to sleep. Instead of waiting until you are crawling into bed, begin the transition period at dinnertime and give yourself a head start.

> *Bless this food to nourish my body and restore my mind.*
> *Bless this food to nourish my mind and restore my body.*
> *Bless this food to replenish my energy as I ease into repose.*
> *This day, not yet complete, has taken and given.*
> *Help this food to restore my depleted energy.*

*Help this food to ground me as I recharge.*
*Bless this food and bless me.*

This blessing reminds you to allow yourself the time to recuperate your energy. We live in a society that tells us to "go, go, go" all the time. Slowing down, recharging, and taking the rest we need is part of what gets us to—and keeps us at—our optimum selves.

## Healing Blessing

Whether you suffer from chronic pain or a broken heart, blessing your food with curative energies helps you to release what ails you and work on healing your body and soul. This blessing works with your breathing as you inhale positive healing vitality and exhale negativities. Add green or blue candles to help build your healing energy.

Before you say the blessing, close your eyes and take three deep breaths. As you inhale, visualize positive energy flowing in through your nose. Let it lift away negative energy wherever it is stored inside of your body and then exhale it out loudly with a woosh through your mouth.

*Bless this food to bring me healing grace.*
*Mend my [insert issue].*
*Mend my spirit.*
*Mend my soul.*

Take another deep breath in and out slowly. Repeat the phrase above, followed by another deep inhalation and exhalation for a total of three times. Finish with your closing. This blessing works with the power of your visualizations and relaxing your body to help the healing begin.

Remember, spells, blessings, and other workings don't necessarily have to be long to be powerful. When you are working with fewer words, it's easier to memorize them and use them repeatedly to build energy. Repetition builds considerable energy easily.

## Energizing Blessing

When you need an extra boost of energy, bless your fuel to work at its most optimal efficiency. With this blessing, you will want to focus on visualizing pulling positive energy from the air around you and sending it through your power (or dominant) hand to your meal or drink.

Hold your nondominant out in front of you or to the side palm up. You will absorb the energy through this hand and then focus and direct it out through your dominant hand, which you will hold, palm down, over your meal or drink.

Yellow and/or orange candles boost the positive energy in the air, as will the scents of lemon, orange, or peppermint.

Visualize the energy cycle of pulling the energy from your atmosphere, through one hand, and out the other as you say:

*From the air I claim the source,*
*Transform the energy and*
*Send it forth.*
*Boost my power,*
*Boost my might,*
*Energize this [food, drink, meal]*
*with vibrancy and light.*

When you must read the words as you say them, it occupies some of your focus. Short and sweet can help you build your power by memorizing the words. Rhyming can also make memorization easier, allowing you to guide your focus more accurately.

## Happiness Blessing

Finding a life that brings you true happiness is often considered the meaning of life. It's also often said anything worth having is worth working for. Life is not easy at times, and finding true happiness can be a long, hard trip with many bumps in the road. But the journey is worth it. We find great moments of bliss along the way, which can help sustain us and even revive us when needed. This blessing directs you to tap into previous moments of happiness to infuse your food with positivity.

When preparing to say this blessing, pull upon memories of joy. Picture them in your mind and recall the way you felt. Allow the feeling to come back to you. Draw on those feelings to create a new energy of cheerful enchantment and direct it into the meal you are blessing by visualizing it flowing from your dominant (or power) hand as you say:

> *Memories of happiness past,*
> *I pull into the present.*
> *The joy they brought me then,*
> *I now use to augment*
> *This meal before me,*
> *Infused with sheer delight.*
> *Take this conjured energy*
> *To disperse in every bite.*

Add candles of your favorite color to your meal to enhance the positive energy.

Building and maintaining a healthy relationship with food makes it easier to build and maintain other positive relationships in your life. This starting point can help you to identify and either mend relationships or end ones that are not in your best interest. This new attitude and respect for food can help you discover new attitudes and respect in other areas of your life. Let it be the beginning of a chain reaction of healing.

# 5
## Bedtime Routines

Getting into a routine of winding down in the evening can help ensure the success of a good night's sleep. A good night's sleep is essential for us to be at the top of our game and for our bodies to be at their best. To function, we need rest. It is a simple fact. Getting good sleep is often difficult for many people.

When we are children, our parents help us to establish a routine at night that is designed to help us shift from day-time extroverted energy to a calmer, introverted energy, which helps us drift off to sleep. As we get older, we often put these routines aside. The problem is, these kinds of routines work, and yet we neglect them. They work because our bodies have a natural energy cycle called the circadian rhythm that works in conjunction with other natural energy cycles, especially the rise and fall of the sun. When we do not work with our body's natural energy cycle and instead work against it, we obviously aren't performing at an optimal level.

Reintroduce yourself to a nighttime routine. Shut off the TV, shut off the computer or tablet, put the phone down. Try some relaxing yoga. Prepare everything you need for the next day. Take a bath, read a book, read a book in the bath. Play relaxing music, use candlelight, diffuse relaxing oils, or light incense. When it's time to go to bed, be relaxed and ready to go to sleep.

Everyone has a different schedule. My mornings don't usually start until 9:00 or 10:00 a.m. That is because I don't usually go to sleep until between 2:00 and 4:00 a.m. I fought my body for a long time and would try to go to bed at 10:00 p.m. All that would happen is I would lie there hour after hour after hour unable to sleep. I finally gave up and decided to listen to my body instead. If I can't sleep, I might as well be doing something constructive, and so now, most of my writing is done in the middle of the night after everyone else in the house has gone to bed and I can work uninterrupted. I do have a nighttime routine; I just start it later than most people do.

## Get It All Down

Take time as you are winding down for the night to prepare everything you need for the next day. Set alarms. Update your affirmation board. Spend time reading through any upcoming meditations or workings that you need to start preparing for. Make lists of the things you need to do for the next day;

make lists of supplies you need. Update as necessary. Take the time for any journal writings you need to do. Check in with your calendar. This is time for you to get everything prepared for yourself for later. Giving yourself this time to prepare and center not only your practice but also your life is another act of self-care people don't necessarily think about. It is a commitment to yourself to ensure your bases are covered and your work is done efficiently. Giving yourself prep time can help eliminate stress and anxiety in the future.

 ## Journal Exercise

Spend a few days documenting your evening and how you wind down and get ready for bed. Next, review what you wrote and evaluate what actions you currently take to help yourself make this shift and any you take that are counterproductive to a good night's sleep. Do you have a routine or is every night more played by ear? What changes can you make to ensure you are getting the best rest possible? Begin making changes, one or two at a time for several days and then add in more if you need to. Always give yourself several days to begin building new habits before adding more changes on top of them. Making a few changes over a longer period of time is generally more successful than making a bunch of changes all at once.

# Bedtime Meditations

These meditations can help you wind down your day, help you evaluate different aspects of your day, and of course, a body scan before bed is always an excellent idea. Depending on how your day went, different days will require different methods and meditations for decompressing. Choose which workings best meets your needs.

## EVALUATE THE DAY AND FILE IT AWAY

One of the reasons it can be so difficult to turn off your mind before bed is because you have had all these different things happen to you throughout the day, and your brain is looking for a way to compartmentalize it all. It needs to sort things out and store them away. Give it the chance to with this meditation.

Begin by closing your eyes and taking a few deep breaths. When you think back over the day, what immediately stands out to you? Take a moment to think about and evaluate the situation. Was it a positive, negative, or neutral experience? Was this event something you will need to contend with again later, or is it over and done? Don't get caught up in details of an event. Don't attempt to relive it. All you want to do is look at it objectively and decide where you would like to store it for now. Take an inventory and pack it away. Visualize yourself sorting these events out and filing them where they belong. Trifles can be tossed into a garbage can. Important information can be locked into a safe. Issues from work can be left on top of a desk as you walk away. Once you pack away the things that come to you right away, scan back over the day, from the beginning to the present. Does anything else catch your attention? If not, that is fine. If there are still moments, conversations, or issues that arise, continue asking yourself, "Where do I want to store this for now?" and then go ahead and visualize yourself putting it there. When you are done sorting and storing, tell yourself they are put away for the night. They are not coming back out. Everything can wait until it is time for them to be dealt with. Until then, they are put on hold and need not bother you. Remember, the more you tell yourself something, the truer it becomes.

When everything is packed away, go about your bedtime routine as normal.

## BEDTIME BODY SCAN

Bedtime body scans are especially beneficial for people who suffer from chronic pain. If you want to add a scent to the air or play some music, set it up and get into bed, lying flat with your head on your pillow. You may cover with your blankets if you want. Close your eyes and relax. Take several deep breaths. Inhale for a count of five, hold for a count of five, and exhale for a count of five.

Begin with your toes, curling and uncurling them, stretching them out as far as possible. Flex and bend the foot a few times followed by rotating the ankles in both directions.

Make a note of any pain you come across, recognize it, and for now, move on to the next body area. Tighten and relax your calf muscles. Bend your knees by putting your feet flat on your bed and sliding them closer to you. Let your knees fall first to one side and then the other. Bring them to center again and straighten them back out. Tighten your core muscles and let them relax. Continue scanning for any issues as you go. Wiggle your fingers, stretch them out far apart and then close them down into a tight fist before relaxing. Lift your shoulders toward your ears and release. Turn your head both left and right; raise your chin high into the air and then pull it in again close to your chest.

If you find any issues, use this knowledge to make sleep more comfortable by arranging pillows, bolsters, or blankets in a way that gives your body more support where needed. If you don't find any issues—great! Your body is ready for a good night's sleep. Give it one.

## NIGHTTIME MENTAL RELAXATION

Night comes and our bodies are ready to rest—but sometimes our minds miss the memo. This is a simple mindfulness meditation to help calm the restless thoughts that may keep you up at night. Begin this meditation when you are fully ready to go to sleep.

As you are lying down, whether on your back, side, stomach—whichever position is most comfortable for you—find a spot to hold your gaze for a few moments. This can be done in the dark as well, as you want to look at something that is not moving. A spot on the ceiling, a picture on the wall. Avoid gazing on something that moves such as a ceiling fan that is turned on or a clock. Once you choose something to gaze upon, take a slow, deep breath in. With the exhale, gently blink your eyes. Inhale a second time, slowly blinking on the exhale. Repeat this process for ten breaths, leaving your eyes closed on the tenth exhale.

Now that your eyes our closed, notice what thoughts come up. Take this time to practice acknowledging and releasing each thought. Did your grocery list come up? Tell that thought, "Okay, I've acknowledged you and now I release you until tomorrow." By actively letting go of each thought, you are emptying your mind. You may find that many thoughts come up during this time, and that is okay. Acknowledge each thought—it is there for a reason—and then release it; let it go.

This mindfulness practice may take time, and some nights may be easier than others. Building a continuous, regular practice will help you develop the skills needed to truly relax for a restful sleep.

## LET IT GO MEDITATION

While the song "Let it Go" raged in popularity among children, the title is also a message many adults can benefit from. We often have a difficult time letting go. We hold on to an outdated image of ourselves. We hold on to bad habits. We hold on to feelings we don't know how to deal with. We hold on to many things that are not good for us. Change isn't easy and it requires work. That work often starts with letting go. Use this meditation on the tough days. The days when something bad happens and the feeling follows you around. While this meditation won't solve your problems for you, it will help you clear your head to be able to better deal with the issue at hand when you are ready. It will allow you to let go of the negativity that makes it difficult to achieve a good, stress-free night of sleep.

You can do this meditation while either lying in bed or sitting somewhere comfortably before getting into bed.

Close your eyes and take several deep breaths. Focus on your breathing. Feel the air as it fills your lungs. Blow the air out through your mouth in as heavy a sigh as you can muster. Really let it go. Visualize you are expelling every last bit of air in your lungs and then refilling them completely.

Wrap both of your arms around yourself in a tight hug and hold it while you continue to breathe in and out as deeply as you can. Focus only on your breath. Any thoughts that come up, blow them out when you exhale and think to yourself, "Let it go." Let them all go. Let all other thoughts go and focus only on your inhalations and exhalations. In and out. You will feel a change, a release that takes place. This release may be accompanied with tears. That is perfectly fine and even ideal. Crying is an incredible release for pent-up tension and anxiety. If tears do fall, let them. Don't attempt to hold back; there is no need to. Let it all go.

When you are ready, let go of your self-hug. Take a few more breaths, allowing them to become shallower and back to your normal rhythm with each cycle. Be at peace and go to sleep.

# Bedtime Affirmations

Affirmations at bedtime help you unwind, relax, and get a good night's sleep. They help keep you in a positive frame of mind. Choose an affirmation from these that will serve your purpose for the night.

## WINDING DOWN

These affirmations help you switch gears and slow down at the end of the day.

* I am at peace. I am ready for rest.
* I am calm. I am serene. I am in harmony with the universe.
* I rest to begin again.
* I welcome the peace of the night. I welcome serene sleep.
* I am ready to reset myself with sleep.
* I deserve rest. I am designed for it.
* I am worthy of a restful night's sleep.
* I am thankful for the opportunities I received today.

* I look forward to tomorrow; I say goodnight to today.

* Each night I say goodbye to an old me and say hello to a new me.

## I AM ENOUGH

Use one of these affirmations to remind yourself you are precisely who you need to be. Life is a journey with many stops along the way.

* I am well. I am loved. I am whole.

* I am right where I need to be.

* I am resilient.

* I accept and love who I am.

* I believe in myself.

* I am a work in progress.

* I am me, and that is all I need to be.

* I am worthy.

* I am everything that I need.

* I have respect for myself, others, and nature.

## RELEASE

When you have a difficult day, it is important to release the negative thoughts and energies before going to bed. Use one of these affirmations to help you let go when needed.

* I release what does not serve me.
* I release myself from expecting perfection.
* I release myself from my own negative judgments.
* I let go of worry. I let go of self-doubt. I am okay. I am me.
* I am not the mistakes I have made.
* I forgive myself.
* Today does not determine tomorrow.
* I let go and let be.
* I release the stress of the day.
* I choose to rest at ease. Worries are set aside.
* I acknowledge my mistakes.

## ACKNOWLEDGING THE POSITIVE

Just as important as letting go of the negative is acknowledging the positive. Choose one of these affirmations when the situation fits.

* Today, I achieved great things.
* Today, I tried my best.
* I am determined and capable.
* I find the silver lining.
* I am comfortable with myself.
* I trust myself.

* I am warm. I am safe. I am protected.
* I am proud of myself today.
* I am my priority. My peace is my priority.

## GROOVY MYSTICAL

Projecting an ethereal or spiritual atmosphere before bed can help deepen your spirituality and your connection to deity or the universe, and it can assist in dream work. These affirmations can help you set the mood.

* I listen to my intuition.
* I dream of wonder and hope.
* I am mindful and present.
* I look forward to my dreams.
* I am love. I am peace. I am the universe.
* I surround myself with love.
* I deserve peace. I deserve rest. I deserve me.
* I grow each day.
* I am the light in my own life.
* I accept and love myself for who I am.

Affirmations can be done while getting ready for bed, lying in bed, during an evening wind-down yoga routine, or in any other way you want. What speaks to you? I like to do nighttime affirmations in front of my altar while sitting on a meditation cushion. I set a mirror up on my altar, light an appropriate candle, and recite my affirmations into the mirror. Looking yourself in the eye as you say them adds a whole other level of energy. It becomes more than an affirmation; it becomes a commitment to the self.

## Bedtime Prayers

If you work with a higher power, you may want to say a prayer of thankfulness and appreciation at the end of the day and ask for protection through the night. Bedtime prayers do not belong to any one religion or pathway. You are welcome and able to speak with your higher power whenever you want to or feel a need to, no matter who your higher power is. Open and close your prayers in the manner that works for you.

### PROTECTION BEDTIME PRAYER

This prayer is not only easy to learn but also a quick way to ask for protection and peace throughout the night, while putting any negative feelings left from the day aside.

*As I lay me down to sleep*
*I ask my [lady / lord / deity] to keep me safe.*
*Grant me strength, grant me peace.*
*Any negativity, I release.*
*Fill my heart with love and grace,*
*Protect me in your sacred space.*
*Shelter me throughout the night,*
*And wake me with your morning light.*

When you say this prayer, visualize your deity casting a protective bubble around you in which you are protected and safe.

## DREAM WORK PRAYER

Use this prayer for inviting your deities or higher spirits to send you a lesson through the dreamworld for dream workings. Remember, if you have a difficult time memorizing, you can write your prayers down on cards to keep next to your bed for easy access.

> *Through the dark I rest my eyes*
> *While my dreams help me to realize,*
> *Messages sent through the night*
> *Can help me find the path of right.*
> *You know what I am ready for,*
> *I trust you won't send any more.*
> *Bring me visions to help me grow,*
> *Show me what I need to know.*
> *In the morning, when I open my eyes,*
> *Let me remember where my mind flies.*

As with spells, intention is also an important factor when it comes to prayer. When you become more proficient in learning from your dreams and you are emotionally ready, this is an excellent prayer to use with shadow dream work, as you can use your intention to bring you what you need to heal. Dreams can be a safe place for uncovering distressing information. However, dreams can also be a scary place for uncovering distressing information. Using this prayer before dream work helps to set up a safe environment. You will learn more about shadow work in chapter 8.

## PRAYER FOR HEALING

When we need healing in our lives, we need to learn to ask our higher power for assistance. Asking for help isn't always easy, and many people have been taught asking for help is a sign of weakness. It is not. It is a sign of knowing your own capabilities and limits. It is a sign of self-care. There is no shame in asking for help. The real shame is how people have been taught they need to be strong 100 percent of the time with no help from anyone. It is an unrealistic expectation designed to make people feel like failures. We have set ourselves and others up with impossible goals of perfection. We are now learning to do better. Asking for help is a sign of a healing individual.

As always, begin this prayer by addressing your higher power in a manner that is comfortable for you and then continue:

> *I call upon [name] to send me aid and healing,*
> *which I need.*
> *Stand by me through my suffering,*
> *Help me shoulder this load.*

Take a moment here to use your own words to describe what burden you carry. Is it emotional? Physical? Describe your ailment. What do you need to heal? Take as much time as you want to express what healing you need. Don't worry about it sounding "just right." Relax. Imagine you are having a conversation with a beloved, trusted friend. After all, you are. When you are ready, continue:

> *I come to you, with reverence, honor, and love,*
> *And ask for your aid.*
> *Help me to heal.*
> *Pick me up when I am down.*
> *Hold me strong when I am weak.*
> *Show me light in the darkness.*
> *Share your strength when I call.*
> *Share your compassion if I fall.*

End your prayer in your normal manner.

The word "fall" in this prayer refers to the stumbles we make while in the process of healing—whether literally or figuratively. Healing comes with setbacks, as it isn't always a straightforward well-lit road. Sometimes the pathway to healing is dark with unexpected twists and turns. Falling is just another obstacle along life's journey and often comes with lessons we need to learn. Society teaches us to look at setbacks as negative, but often they lead to a different, better solution than what was originally planned. A turn in the road is neither a positive nor a negative. It is just a turn in the road, which temporarily leads us in a different direction than what we expected. These side roads are still a part of our overall journey of life. How we learn to adapt to them is evidence of growth and enlightenment.

## PRAYER OF GRATITUDE AND THANKFULNESS

One of the best ways to find yourself in a more positive state of mind is to accentuate the positive over the negative. Focusing on negative feelings gives them energy. This isn't to say we ignore them—not at all. We learn to process them, learn from them, and move on. But, if we focus too much on the negative, we risk allowing it to overshadow the positive. Taking our time to give a prayer of gratitude and thankfulness at the end of the day brings the focus to all that we have and are. Not only is it a wonderful spiritual practice to be mindful of and thankful for what you have, but it also puts your mind in a happy, grateful state before going to sleep.

Open your prayer as normal and then continue:

*As this day comes to an end*
*I thank you for all you send.*
*I am grateful for all I have,*
*I am grateful for all I am.*
*I have joy in my life,*
*And as I go to sleep this night,*
*I remind myself of all that is right.*

Take time to list your blessings. What are the best parts of your life? What are you proud of? What brings a smile to your face? What was the best part of your day? After listing what comes to mind, close your prayer as normal.

Remember, it's not only about the big moments in life. Each day brings us some sort of positivity. Sometimes the positive might be difficult to find, but it is there. Finding the good and giving thanks for what you have is an effective way to calm the mind and put yourself into a better state before drifting off to sleep.

In the last few chapters, we have worked on analyzing our current patterns and setting up new daily routines that help incorporate more spirituality and positivity into our life. Throughout the rest of this book, we will cover spells, rituals, and other workings to help you through difficult times while boosting self-love and self-esteem.

# 6
## Workings for Self-Esteem

For months now, I have been hearing from Pagans, witches, and other people that they suddenly feel like their eyes have been opened and they are seeing things differently. While some people call this being "woke," it truly is a type of enlightenment. When you feel a veil has been lifted from your eyes and you see things from a different point of view, you are experiencing a side effect of enlightenment.

With the emergence of the great awakening, many people are learning new truths about themselves. This truth often includes that we deserve more. We deserve better. We have settled. We have accepted. We have done what we were told, often without question, because "That's the way it's always been done." Sometimes, we also discover we have been wrong about things. Being wrong is okay. It means we have the opportunity to learn. Awakening to a new truth also means working through it.

We are also realizing (finally!) on a broad scale that the idea of perfection is subjective. One size does not fit all. We do not have to fit into some generic mold. We are not all the same, nor do we all aspire to be the same. We are unique individuals who need to celebrate our differences and learn from them instead of fearing and attempting to control them.

Issues with self-esteem can arise from a variety of causes. We will discuss later how shadow work can help you find causes when they are unknown to you. It is important to remember magical work is always to be backed up with mundane work. Seek a therapist if you need one. Awakening isn't easy work.

The workings we do here are designed to help boost your overall self-esteem. Work through them whenever you need, as often as you need. You can do these before you begin or in conjunction with shadow work.

## Primal Confidence Booster

Whether you find this working silly or deeply serious, either way, it works. You can use it when you need a seriously deep working, or you can use it when you feel like being on the freer, lighter, more fun side of life. Remember to set your intention ahead of time as to what type of an experience you want. Let your inner animal out for a romp or your inner beast out for a hunt.

Your first step is to find a song that will work for you. Something that for you represents a primal, animalistic nature. (Personally, I love "Lion" by Saint Mesa.)

Next, you will need to find a safe private location—indoors, outside, day, night—whatever works best for you, but I do love to do this outside at night when no one will see me anyway. You do not want to be interrupted. You do you.

You will need some way, of course, to play the music—phone, headphones—again, do what works for you. Feel free to set the song to repeat or make a short playlist for this working with a few different songs that work for you.

Go to your location, turn your music on, close your eyes (hence the need for a safe place), and listen. Focus only on the primal aspect of the music. Let it move you. There are no judgments here at all. Move however you want. The old saying, "Dance like no one is watching"? No one is watching. Yourself included. Dance. Crawl. Stalk. Do whatever your instincts tell you to do. Let those primal instincts take control. Don't think about it; just let instinct take over. Move. Growl. Purr. What do you want to do? When you let go and tap into primal energies, you can feel your self-confidence boost. Primal energies do not judge. They are a part of who we are at the most basic level. They are a part of an energy force that has existed since the beginning of time. They are accepting and filled with a positive charge. Primal energies focus on survival; they are filled with strength, which you can channel into a boost of confidence.

Letting go can be difficult; don't feel bad if you can't completely do it the first few times. It takes practice. As humans, we are trained to subdue our primal energies. This is a time for you to not only call upon them, but to also explore and use them. Once you can unlock the door that keeps those energies inaccessible, you are able to better understand them. When you access them, you'll know. There is no doubt. The difficulty is in getting there. The key is in your hands, but the correct usage means letting the walls crumble so you can reach the door.

Keep practicing until you succeed. Besides, practicing this is fun; every time you practice, you will get closer to full success, and it helps in the activity department too, giving a natural boost of adrenaline and endorphins, which also boost confidence. Even if you cannot fully tap into the primal energies yet, you are still getting confidence-boosting benefits from each of your attempts.

# Self-Acceptance Ritual

I remember when I was a child, I thought when I was a teenager, I would suddenly feel different. I would gain some sort of insight that would totally alter my personality and make me feel like a different person. When I was a teenager, I thought it would happen in my twenties. In my twenties, I thought it would be my thirties. Eventually, I realized the event I was waiting for wasn't some outside stimulus that would grant me sudden enlightenment. It would take place inside of me.

A true turning inward and seeing myself through the eyes of others instead of my own. It wouldn't be instantaneous either. Turns out, it can take a whole lot of work to find out who you really are, particularly if you are recovering from trauma or are suffering from trauma you have not yet realized.

What is important to remember is this: You are who you are. No matter who that is, you are worthy of love. You are capable of love. You are an important part of the universe. You exist for a purpose. Whether you know and comprehend your purpose or not, it is okay. You have one, and you will find it when you are ready.

No matter where you are on your journey, you are right where you are supposed to be when you are supposed to be there. Your journey is specific to you.

In this ritual, you will work on embracing who you are at this point in your life. This is a ritual you can do many times over. Every new lesson you learn, every new experience you have, combine to create slight changes in who you are, so every time you repeat the ritual, you will be a different person than the time before. Ideally, you should perform it on (or right around) the full moon. You can make this part of a monthly practice, with each ritual an acknowledgment of your growth from the previous one.

For this ritual you will need:

* A mirror
* White spell-size candle

* Pink spell-size candle

* Holders for both candles

* A lighter or matches

If you work with an altar, you may want to set your candles and mirror up on it. You will want to be able to sit either on the ground or in a chair and see clearly into the mirror. Place the unlit candles in between your seat and the mirror, with the white candle to the left and the pink candle to the right.

Seat yourself to look in the mirror, close your eyes, and take a few deep breaths to ground and center yourself. Put other thoughts aside. Focus your attention on yourself. Open your eyes.

Say:

> *By the light and the power of the full moon,*
> *I celebrate all that I am.*

Light the white candle.
Say:

> *I have compassion for who I am.*
> *I have love for who I am.*
> *I accept who I am.*

Light the pink candle.

Gaze deeply into the mirror, into your own eyes, in between the two flames.

As you gaze, continue to chant, "*I accept who I am.*" Find a cadence that works for you. I usually prefer to chant more slowly in a whispered tone when it has been a month of rougher trials, tribulations, or revelations. Other months, I find myself in a more positive state of mind, and at those times, a more jubilant, energetic chant is called for. Use what works for you, but be sure to experiment so that you experience the different energies you can create. Continue your chant until your candles burn down or you feel you are ready to extinguish them. Some traditions teach snuffing out candles to keep the energy contained, while others believe in blowing out the candles to send the energy to the universe. I am of the second belief system, but you do what feels natural to you. Simply be safe either way.

We all have work to do on ourselves. Anyone who tells you they don't most likely has the most of all. We never stop learning. We never stop growing. Not in this lifetime, nor the next. Think of this ritual as a monthly stepping-stone. Check in with yourself and celebrate who you are and where you are on your lifelong journey.

## Forgiving Others

Always remember, giving forgiveness is not giving permission. It is not giving permission for someone to treat you in the same way again. It is not giving permission for the person to have access to your life if you don't want them to. Forgiveness does not mean you condone their actions. Forgiveness does not have to mean "it's okay" if it really is not okay. You can decide what terms are set when forgiving someone. You are allowed to forgive them and still tell them to get lost. You are allowed to forgive them and keep them in your life. You have the right to decide. You may also decide not to decide now what you want to do in the future, but know your heart is ready for forgiveness.

This exercise is a multipart working. In the first step, you will need to spend some time (think days, possibly weeks, not minutes), writing down who you want to forgive and why. It is often easier to forgive those who have harmed us than it is to forgive our own selves, so you will start there. You also want to clear out of your life any unfinished business with others. This will allow you to devote more time and energy to yourself. It is something you may have to do every now and then—anytime there is a reason in your life to forgive someone else and move on. The first time you do this, however, expect to come up with a longer list than subsequent workings. Take your time and use your words and feelings to get it all down on paper. What was the situation? What was the outcome? Is it fixable?

Write down everything you would like to say to the people involved. Giving forgiveness may involve people that are no longer here. Are there people who have passed away whom you are working on forgiving? Getting your feelings out of your mind and heart down onto paper is a healing act.

You can envision removing pain as you write. Each time you add something new to your list, another burden is lifted. When we do not give forgiveness, the offending action and offender still hold a power over us. When we release ourselves from this power, we feel lighter, relieved, and less burdened. We do not have to continue to suffer from the wrongs of others. We can forgive and move on. Again, forgiving and forgetting are two different things, and it is up to you on how you decide to proceed after forgiveness is given.

Once you have your list complete and are ready to move on, you can start the next part of this working.

For this ritual you will need:

* A large enough area outside where you can sit down and form a protective circle around yourself

* A fireproof container large enough to burn the pages you have written. This may be a cauldron you burn in, a fire pit or bonfire, or even a charcoal grill. (Do not burn things inside of a gas grill.)

* A lighter

* 4 white candles

* Representations of earth, air, fire, water placed in their respective elemental locations (east: air, south: fire, west: water, north: earth)

* As many lavender buds as you want to use
* Moon water (prepared ahead of time)
* A shovel or small trowel
* Dirt or salt (This will have a symbolic meaning, so do not worry if you do not have a lot.)
* Representations of your deities if you wish to use them
* Soft, soothing music
* You may want something such as a meditation cushion to sit on to ensure comfort while you work.

To begin, set the 4 white candles in the circle around you at the halfway points between each direction (southwest, southeast, northwest, northeast), allowing them to complete the circle around you.

You may place the lavender and your papers anywhere inside the circle that works for you.

Take a few moments to center and ground yourself. Relax. Take a few deep breaths and focus your attention on the task at hand.

Don't be afraid or ashamed to show emotion. Forgiveness can trigger a variety of feelings. Working through, letting out, and then letting go of difficult emotions is exhausting both emotionally and physically. However, it helps the healing process move along.

Beginning by facing east (unless your tradition states otherwise). Call upon the earthly energies of each direction and ask them to join with you:

*I call upon the energies of the east.*
*May the power of air come to me and aid me in*
*my quest.*

Light the candle at southeast before turning to face south.

*I call upon the energies of the south.*
*May the power of fire come to me and aid me in*
*my quest.*

Light the candle at southwest before turning to face west.

*I call upon the energies of the west.*
*May the power of water come to me and aid me in*
*my quest.*

Light the candle at northwest before turning to face north.

*I call upon the energies of the north.*
*May the power of earth come to me and aid me in*
*my quest.*

Light the candle at northeast and find yourself a comfortable location to sit in the circle.

Call upon your deity by saying:

*I call upon [name] to guide me,*
*To walk with me and comfort me.*

Take a few more deep breaths and relax before continuing with the following.

> *I call upon these energies and [name(s) of deities]*
> *As I am ready to forgive and move on with my life.*
> *I have felt anger, hurt, pain.*
> *It is time for me to put those aside.*
> *To return these negative energies to the universe to*
> *be cleansed, recycled, converted into something new.*
> *I release those who have hurt me from the pain*
> *they have caused.*
> *I release any anger,*
> *I release any hurt,*
> *I release any pain.*
> *It serves no purpose for me.*
> *I ask the energies of the earth:*
> *Air, release a cleansing breeze to wash the negative*
> *energy away.*
> *Fire, I give to you these offerings of my pain.*
> *Burn them away. Take the negative energy away.*

Set your papers on fire and allow them to burn. As they burn, sprinkle bits of lavender so it burns with them. Visualize the negative energy going up in the lavender smoke. Watch it go—the lavender releasing its own energy to cleanse the negativity away. It is released by the fire to be reabsorbed into the universe, converted to neutral energy, stored away like a battery for later use. When they are done burning, continue.

> *Water, wash away and cleanse any negativity*
> *that remains.*

Using a bit of the moon water, first bless yourself on the forehead to wash away and cleanse any negativity that remains there. Do the same with your heart next. Finally, pour some of the water on the ashes of the pages you burned. With each action you perform, visualize the water washing away any negativity that may remain. With this action, your forgiveness becomes complete.

> *Earth, ground the energy. Restore it to*
> *the universe.*

Scatter either the dirt or the salt over the ashes. Visualize the energy grounding, becoming neutral until it is called upon to act in another time, in another place. With this action, you release yourself from the pain. You have grounded the energy, taking away its negative power. Use this time to sink in and let any emotions out that you need to. If you want to cry, this is the time to do it. Let all the negative energy seep away into the ground underneath you. The earth knows what to do with it. Let her do her work. When you are ready to move on, say the following:

> *I forgive because I am strong, not out of weakness.*
> *I forgive to not carry a burden which isn't mine.*

*I forgive to heal myself.*
*I forgive to love me.*

You may continue in a meditative state for as long as you would like. When you are ready to close, thank and release your higher power(s).

*[Deity name(s)], thank you for your guidance, for*
*protecting me and surrounding me with your love.*

Turn to the east and say:

*To the east and the energy of air,*
*I thank you for your cleansing breeze.*
*I thank you for your power and release you.*

Blow out the candle at the southeast as you turn to face south. Say:

*To the south and energy of fire,*
*I thank you for your cleansing flame.*
*I thank you for your power and release you.*

Blow out the candle at the southwest as you turn to face west and say:

*To the west and energy of water,*
*I thank you for your cleansing droplets.*
*I thank you for your power and release you.*

Blow out the candle at the northwest as you turn to face north and say:

> *To the north and energy of earth,*
> *I thank you for your grounding dirt.*
> *I thank you for your power and release you.*

Blow out the candle at the northeast and say:

> *I have forgiven.*
> *I am healed.*
> *I am whole.*
> *So mote it be.*

After finishing this working, do some grounding by lying on the earth and allowing it to absorb your extra energy. Another favorite way of mine to ground that my group and I joke about frequently is eating cheese. A good hunk of cheese does wonders for grounding.

## Self-Forgiveness Ritual

Sometimes we do things that we regret; to make a mistake is the most human thing that we do. Whether we receive forgiveness from others or not, it is important to look within and offer that forgiveness to ourselves. Forgiving yourself is an important step in the inner healing process. As we forgive, we are relieved of a heaviness that may have been holding us back. This relief allows us to step forward to a brighter future.

For this ritual, we will craft an herbal incense blend used for self-forgiveness. We will use garden sage for inner healing and to promote wisdom and longevity. Hyssop is used to cleanse, purify, and lighten our vibrations. Rosemary assists with memory and focus. Basil brings luck, softens tensions, and heals rifts. These herbs can be charged before your ritual by holding on to each one, closing your eyes, and focusing on the intentions mentioned here. Once charged, place the herbs in a small dish on your altar until they are needed in the ritual.

This ritual can be done either indoors with a potted plant or jar of dirt or outdoors where you can connect directly with the earth by using the soil in your yard.

For this working you will need:

* Paper and pen
* Access to soil (outdoors, a potted plant, or a jar of dirt)
* Garden shovel
* Cauldron or fireproof dish
* Charcoal tablet
* Lighter or matches
* 1 teaspoon garden sage
* 1 teaspoon hyssop
* 1 teaspoon rosemary

* 1 teaspoon basil

* A small dish (to hold the herbs listed above)

Before beginning this ritual, take time to center yourself. Self-forgiveness can be an emotional exercise, so it is best to be prepared in advance and take some extra deep breaths. When you are ready, activate the charcoal tablet by lighting it until it sparks and ignites. Using your pen and paper, write the following:

> *I forgive myself for . . .*

Finish the sentence; be as detailed as possible. It is important to be completely honest and authentic as you write. Take note of how these words make you feel but release any judgment you may be experiencing. Admitting to all your wrongdoings is key to truly moving forward. Take ownership for your actions. As you write, reflect on how the situation made you feel and what thoughts went through your head at that time.

Once you have finished writing, fold the piece of paper toward you three times and then recite:

> *I have made mistakes.*
> *I take ownership for my actions.*
> *I am deserving of forgiveness.*
> *I forgive myself for the wrong that I have done.*

Now, you will fold the paper away from you three times. Afterward, recite the following:

> *I release this burden so that I may move forward.*

Set the paper down in the center of your altar. The herbs listed in the ingredients will be used now as an incense. Carefully add the herbs to the charcoal tablet—this can be done one at a time or mixed in the bowl and added all at once, whichever you prefer. As the herbal incense burns, take your self-forgiveness note and weave it in and out of the smoke, returning your focus to your intentions of forgiving yourself.

Next, it is time to bury the note. If indoors, a potted plant or jar of soil or dirt will do. If outdoors, you can use the dirt in your yard. Prepare your jar or planter, or dig a hole in the earth. Place the note inside and bury it beneath the soil. Press the soil down on top and repeat the following one last time:

*I forgive myself for the wrong that I have done.*
*I release this burden so that I may move forward.*

To finish this ritual, close your eyes. Wrap your arms around yourself in a tight embrace and bow your head slightly downward. Picture a healing, light energy filling you from within, washing away your burden and enveloping you in warmth. Take as much time here as you need, honoring yourself and sending love within.

When you feel ready, release your embrace and take a few deep, cleansing breaths. Allow the herbal incense to burn out on its own fully. (You can leave it outside if you need to if it is in a safe place and will not be disturbed.) Come back to the cauldron or fireproof container after the herbs and charcoal have burnt out and the container is cooled. You can release the ash to the earth or wash it away—whatever feels best for your practice.

At this point, it is time to move forward. After completing this ritual, you cannot dwell on the past. It is time to continue living your life.

## I Am the Only Me

You are a unique, awesome, totally wonderful, and delightful human being. There is no one else out there in the world just like you. There is no one else who has lived your life, has had your experiences, learned your lessons, or felt your emotions. No one else has touched the lives of the people you have in the ways you have. You and only you. In this world of billions of people, no one else is just like you. That makes you incredibly special. Sometimes you need to remind yourself of this fact.

In this ritual, you will be celebrating all the things that make you, you. Spend time planning this out. This shouldn't be rushed. Collect items, pictures, words printed out or cut from magazines, souvenirs, and other keepsakes or mementos that have significant meaning for you—things that are associated with who you are as a person. All these items should be used to decorate your altar. If you need to use a different location than normal for your altar, that's okay; you will be able to take it down afterward. If you need to use the dining room table, then use the dining room table. Be sure to include the other items you would normally use on your altar such as deity statues or elemental representations. Give this deep consideration. This is a shrine to yourself. How can you best represent the parts of yourself you want to celebrate? What traits and qualities do you want to express about yourself?

Add candles to your altar. Choose colors that speak to you or hold special significance. Check out candles in different shapes and figures too. Madame Pamita's Parlour of Wonders has the most incredible variety of beeswax figural candles, from apples to owls, in their online store.

Make this altar as much of a representation of yourself as you can. This is your time to celebrate everything that makes you the special individual you are. Spending the time to contemplate and evaluate the representations you want to include gives you an opportunity to compile a checklist of who you feel you are. Top off your altar by honoring yourself with your favorite incense or diffused oil if you wish. Enrich your atmosphere with a playlist of songs that have meaning to you—a soundtrack of who you are.

When your altar is prepared and you are ready to perform your ritual, dress in an outfit that has significance to you. It can be as serious, casual, or flamboyant as you want. This is all for you!

It can be difficult to focus your attention so deeply on yourself. You may feel like you do not deserve the attention, but you do. If you feel this way, this is something you should address in your shadow work. For now, however, do your best to soak in your own limelight.

If you are using incense and candles, light them.

Take a moment to center yourself and then say:

*Today, I celebrate a wonderful person.*
*A person who has seen good times and bad,*
*Happy times and sad.*
*A person who has loved, a person who has lost.*
*A person who is healing and who is finding*
*[themself/herself/himself].*
*I am the only me. There is no one else like me.*

Look over your altar at all the items you collected. Meditate for as long as you want on their significance to you. How do they represent you? What are your favorite parts of yourself? What do you like about yourself? These are the feelings you want to hold on to. These are the things that make you who you are. These are the things that make you unique. If you want to, write the answers to these questions in your journal. Do not let your mind wander to who you want to be; you are celebrating who you are right now in this moment of life. It has taken a long time to get where you are. You have overcome obstacles in your way. Appreciate the path you have traveled for where it has brought you so far.

When you are ready to continue, say:

*I am unique. I am my own person. There is no one
else like me.*

*I accept, love, and honor the person I have become.*

*While my journey continues before me,*

*I celebrate the person I am now. Today.*

*Right here, right now,*

*I love and celebrate me.*

Finish your ritual when you are ready by extinguishing your candles. Spend time after this ritual performing self-care that you enjoy—soak in the tub, give yourself a massage, enjoy a favorite drink or meal. Reward yourself with an extra dose of love and appreciation.

## Affirmations to Light Up Your Life

Positivity breeds positivity. Send out what you want to attract back. Fake it till you make it. All pieces of advice that, honestly, are quite similar. We use positive affirmations to help put us in a positive frame of mind when we aren't. Let's be clear here: we don't think so much about feeling better when we are already happy. We are looking to feel better about ourselves and the world around us when we don't. There is a lot of pain and misery and suffering in the world. It can be downright cruel. But we don't give up. We don't give in. We trudge through and carry on. We do so because even though there is pain, misery, suffering, and cruelty in the world, there is also love. There is joy. There is happiness and exhilaration.

There is pleasure, mystery, and adventure. Life is much more than the negative. Unfortunately, we live in a society driven by accentuating the negative. Advertisers tell us everything wrong with us to sell their products to fix our problems. The news, though informative, seldom has "good" news. We are bombarded with negativity daily. It can rub off, but we can protect ourselves and even fight back.

These affirmations are to help you feel better about your life and the world around you, especially when you do not feel at peace. Those moments are when you need to capture and harness positivity the most.

While affirmations can be performed anywhere and anytime (which is a huge bonus) you can also take the time and effort to make your session more significant.

When I have the opportunity, I take a meditation pillow out into either my labyrinth or the woods to do affirmation workings there. I particularly love to do this at night in the dark with incense and candlelight. I can't help but feel a bit more magical doing my workings out in the woods in the middle of the night.

What makes you feel magical? You don't have to be doing a full spell or ritual to bring that magical feeling into your workings; in fact, you probably want to be working toward bringing that magical feeling into everything you do. You can make your affirmation workings as casual or as formal as you desire and mix it up as often as you want. You may only want to say your affirmations a couple of times, or you may want to chant them in trance.

Again, you do what you need.

## I'M ALL THAT

Whether you are a bit on the down side or looking for a boost before a job interview, work your magic to boost your confidence with one (or more) of these affirmations:

* I am strong, I am confident, I am my best. I am strong, I am confident, I am blessed.
* I am intelligent. I am capable. I am confident.
* I draw in confidence. I release all doubt.
* Determination, poise, and spirit. I call all in and do not fear them.
* I pull the energy from around me, I let it in, boldness surrounds me. (You can substitute "boldness" for whatever word works best for you: confidence, tenacity, courage, etc.)

## TURN ON THE GLOW

You are a being of light and energy. You radiate this light and energy to others all around you. When you feel your light is dimming, try these affirmations to brighten up your glow.

* I am stardust. I am energy. I am the brightest light.

* Sunlight and moonbeams, moonlight and sunbeams. Stimulate my glow. (Visualize working with the light from both the sun and moon.)
* I am a part of the light which shines upon the world.
* Brighten my way, brighten my day.
* I kindle the fire within me, flames of illumination to light the world around me.

To add in energy conversion while performing your affirmations, sit or stand in a comfortable position. It may help your visualization process to close your eyes. Hold your hands in a comfortable position with your palms facing any direction away from you. You are going to draw the energy from around you through your palms, and you don't want to suck out your own energy. As you repeat your affirmation, visualize collecting energy from the environment around you. Pull the energy into you through your palms. Feel it enter and travel through your body. Feel it combine with the vibrations of your voice as you say the words. Charge the energy with the words you speak as you release them both into the universe.

## Let the Light Shine In Meditation

The combination of this meditation with these bath salts is to help you accept your own self-love without guilt. Many of us, particularly females, were taught self-love was selfish.

We were not taught to take the time for us. We were taught our role was to please others, not ourselves. It is a big change for people when they learn that self-love is not only okay but also a good, healthy thing. Prepare these bath salts ahead of time so they are ready when you are.

## LET THE LIGHT SHINE IN SELF-LOVE BATH SALTS

For these bath salts you will need:

* 1 cup of any combination of bath salts: Epsom salts, sea salt, pink Himalayan salt
* ½ tablespoon lemon balm
* ½ tablespoon jasmine flowers
* ½ tablespoon thyme
* ½ tablespoon red or pink rose buds or petals
* A bowl and spoon or spatula for mixing
* Any 8 ounce jar with a lid
* Optional: colloidal oatmeal for baths

Combine all the ingredients in a bowl and mix until well combined, then transfer into a jar that has a lid. Depending on how much you choose to use, this mixture should last 4–8 baths.

As you combine the ingredients together, remember to add your energy to those you are working with. What song makes you feel good about yourself? Play it or sing it while you are prepping. Pink candles represent compassionate love.

Add some of their energy by burning one while you work and while you use the salts.

## LET THE LIGHT SHINE IN MEDITATION

This meditation is all about opening yourself up to self-love. It is very easy to shut ourselves off from loving ourselves and treating ourselves with the respect and compassion that we deserve. It is time to throw open the blinds and crack a window to let the light shine in on yourself. With this meditation you will use a closed window as a metaphor for being closed off to self-love. Opening the window in this meditation will allow you to open yourself up to let self-love in.

Sit or lie down comfortably in your self-love bath and begin this practice by closing your eyes. Picture yourself in a room inside a house, where the windows are covered with old, dark curtains. This could be someplace familiar and comforting to you, or a new place that you created with your imagination. Look around, notice the details. What is it about this room that is comforting to you? How do you feel when you look around; what feelings, thoughts, and memories come up? These are things you may want to make a mental note of to reflect on later; for now, release these thoughts.

Turn your attention to the windows in the room. How many are there? These represent the layers of walls built up around yourself. What do they look like? How do you feel when you see them? One by one, go to each window. Fling open the curtains, wipe away the dust, and push the window open. Allow the sun to shine in, brightening and warming the room and brightening and warming you. Notice how you feel as you open each window. Imagine a warm breeze blowing through the window, cleansing the room around you. Continue this way until all of the windows are open and the room is filled with a bright, warm light.

Once your windows are open, return to the present moment, keeping your eyes closed. Now that you have opened the window to allow self-love in, end this practice with some self-love breathing. As you take a few slow, deep breaths, wrap your arms around your body in a warm embrace. With each inhale, focus on filling yourself with compassion and kindness, allowing any negativity to be banished with the exhale. Take as much time as you need here. Breathe in compassion and exhale any self-judgment. Breathe in kindness and exhale any negativity. Breathe in self-love and exhale, releasing any heaviness you feel within.

When you are ready, open your eyes. After completing this practice, it is important to spend some time writing about the experience in a journal. Revisit the thoughts, feelings, and memories that came up during the meditation. Reflect on what you were feeling and why these things came up. What do they have to do with self-love? What can you learn from this experience? Continue writing as much as you need to without overthinking it—letting the words flow freely allows you to tap into your intuition and hidden feelings. This is important for healing and moving forward with an open heart.

After this exercise, it is important to remember that self-love is an ongoing practice. This is not something that you do once and move on. You may repeat this meditation as often as you need to, or even just return to the self-love breathing. Self-love practices should be a part of our weekly and even daily routines. Remember, you deserve to love yourself.

# Courage Meditation

Change and fear of the unknown are frightening. Courage is the ability to do something which frightens you. Courage therefore doesn't mean you do something without fear—it means you do it despite the fear. These bath soaks combined with this meditation work together to help you set your fear aside and let your gumption shine through.

## COURAGE BATH SALTS

For these bath salts you will need:

* 1 cup of any combination of bath salts: Epsom salts, sea salt, pink Himalayan salt

* ½ tablespoon borage

* ½ tablespoon fennel

* ½ tablespoon St. John's Wort

* A bowl and spoon or spatula for mixing

* An 8 ounce jar with lid

* Optional: colloidal oatmeal for baths

Combine all the ingredients in a bowl and mix until well combined, then transfer into a jar that has a lid. Depending on how much you choose to use, this mixture should last 4–8 baths.

## COURAGE MEDITATION

Prepare your tub and set your atmosphere. Use black candles to absorb your fears and red candles to boost your courage. Include music that emanates the feeling of power. Add your salts to your water, climb in, and take a few moments to relax with some deep breathing as you let the water warm your muscles.

Close your eyes. Take time to mentally define and describe what your fear is. Think as if you were describing it to a trusted confidant. Break it down as much as you can in your own mind. What is the realistic worst-case scenario if your fear materialized? This is a big step—thinking about and analyzing the worst-case scenario. However, answering "What if?" questions allows both our mind and our body to experience and practice possible triggers while in a safe environment. Go ahead and think to yourself, what if your fear materialized, what is the worst that can happen? Give yourself time to think about and, most importantly, accept the answers you come up with. You may have physical reactions—anxiety, nausea, tears—to some of the responses you come up with. This is okay and expected. It's why we meditate about these things before we do them. We are practicing and allowing our bodies and minds an opportunity to adjust to a change at a slower pace to encourage and promote healing along the way.

Allow yourself to feel and process any negative reactions you have relating to this fear while you are in this safe, warm place. Visualize your fear as a colored energy and watch as it flows from your body and into the water around you. Instead of changing the color of the water, you see it stream like ink as it snakes toward the drain to congregate and hover, trickles slipping down the pipe. Take more deep breaths if needed to let yourself relax. Calm yourself again if necessary.

Exploring worst-case scenarios gives us a great deal of knowledge to work with. When we know different possible outcomes, we can acquire tools or information to minimize unwanted results and boost the likelihood of positive ones instead.

Think about the information you have acquired. You may see something right away that lessens your fear and boosts your courage. If not, that is perfectly fine. You have given yourself material to work with later.

When you are ready, focus your attention back to the drain. Your inky fear is balled up, floating there. Go ahead and pull the plug. Let the fear be sucked right down in a giant gulp.

Exploring your feelings ahead of time lets you know what you are up against. It gives you the opportunity to arm yourself with tools and information to minimize the chances of a worst-case scenario. Fear is a part of what makes courage possible. You understand the risks and proceed anyway.

Having good self-esteem isn't just about liking how you look. It is about accepting who you are as a person. It is realizing and recognizing the value of your self-worth. It is doing the hard work to help heal yourself from past traumas.

It is changing yourself to be the person you want to become.

# 7
## Magic for Coping

$S$ adly, when my generation was younger, we were taught coping was far more about denial than it was about healing. We were told what didn't kill you made you stronger. We were told out of sight, out of mind. We were told if you don't talk about things, they would go away. We were not taught how to cope with things. We were taught how to ignore them and were told that's what "coping" was. There may have been a few families where this was not the norm, but I guarantee you, for most it was. The idea of coping is not the same as it once was.

Today, instead of silence and denial, coping includes the key components of acceptance and healing. The whole idea of mental health is still relatively new, and it is ever evolving. If you read about mental health history, you will find it has travelled a very rocky road at times. Lobotomies and institutionalizations were once considered routine mental health treatment. We've come a long way. We are finally demanding the care and wellbeing for the individual more than ever before, and it is about time.

In this section, we will begin with coping with loss and loneliness and then work on how to rediscover yourself as a part of your healing process.

## Spell for Coping with Loss

For many, a proper goodbye isn't always possible. When this happens, no matter what the circumstances of loss are, it lacks closure. The heart, brain, and soul often need this closure to be able to say goodbye and address the issue of grief. Without the goodbye, there is a sort of limbo where the finality of the situation feels impossible to accept.

Even when there is a chance for a goodbye, it may not have met your needs for closure. It somehow felt incomplete. There may have been more you needed to say but couldn't. With this spell, you can take the time to express the things you wish you had the chance to say to your lost loved one. Find a comfortable place where you will not be interrupted and allow yourself to take as much time as you need.

For this working you will need:

* A white candle

* A firesafe container

* Rosemary

* Lavender
* Pen and paper
* Comfortable seat
* Optional: a photo or token in remembrance of the one you lost
* Optional: an envelope to "mail" your letter in

Allow yourself to sit comfortably and begin by lighting the white candle. Take some time to remember your lost loved one. Look through pictures, touch the tokens you have with you. Picture your loved one in your mind. Imagine they are sitting next to you and think about the things you wish you could say to them. Then, begin to write. Using as many pages as you like, write a letter to your loved one. Tell them how much they mean to you, reminisce with your favorite memories. Tell them about your life today, share happy moments with them. Loss may also trigger feelings of anger. This is okay. Don't hold back any emotions; take this time to fully express yourself.

When you are ready, end your letter and sign your name. Sprinkle the letter with your herbs—rosemary for clarity, remembrance, and cleansing, and lavender for peace, harmony, and healing. Fold the letter, taking care to avoid spilling the herbs, and, if you choose, place it inside of an envelope. Light a corner of the letter with the flame from the white candle, then carefully place it into the fireproof container.

As the letter burns, take as much time as you need to ground yourself. Perhaps enjoy a mug of your favorite beverage. Once the letter has burned, you may scatter the ashes outside in the wind, releasing your words to the universe.

## Coping with Loss Meditation

Address your grief through this meditation, which can be as short or as long as you choose—it is truly up to you. As always, read through the meditation in advance to prepare. In this meditation, you will speak to a loved one that you have lost, so it may be beneficial to prepare some sort of script or letter before sitting down. When you are ready, find a comfortable seat, perhaps set some quiet music in the background, and close your eyes.

As you close your eyes, you are transported to a garden. See it in your mind's eye. Feel the wind blow through your hair, the sun shining on your skin. Smell the flowers and listen to the birds sing. There is a pond in the distance where you can see the reflection of the sun. This is a peaceful place. Know that you are safe here. There is no judgment, only peace.

Ahead of you, there is a picnic. Your loved ones are waiting for you. They are laughing, smiling, talking amongst themselves as they bask in the sunshine and enjoy their favorite foods and beverages. When you are ready, go to them. Join the picnic.

Take this time to truly focus on whatever loved ones you wish to see. Enjoy the time with those that you have lost. Tell them the messages that you wish they would hear. Share stories of your life and hear their words one last time.

When you are ready, it is time to stand up and leave the garden. Say your goodbyes and know that they are always with you, watching over you. They are never truly gone, and they will never be forgotten. Honor the past but do not let it hold you back from moving forward into the future. Life goes on, and it is time to return to live your life.

After you leave the garden and open your eyes, allow yourself the time you need to return to the present. Hold space for yourself. It may be beneficial to journal about your experiences.

## Coping with Loss Affirmations

Affirmations to help you cope with loss can be added into your daily routine or used whenever else they are needed. Choose whichever works best for you.

* I accept that loss is out of my control.
* I accept that grief has changed who I am.
* I am taking my time to grieve.
* Grief is healing. I am healing.
* The pain I feel in my heart will heal.
* To feel loss means I loved, and love is the greatest gift of all.
* I am never alone in my grief. I am loved and supported.

* Grief is temporary. Love is forever.
* I am grateful for the time we were given.
* A soul is never lost. Only energy transformed until we meet again.

We experience different losses in our life—from death to losing a job, home, or friend. All are types of losses, and each will require their own unique journey of healing. The overall theme of loss, however, is universal.

## Coping with Loss Prayer

Speaking with your deities, your guides, your higher self, or the universe helps you to process feelings related to loss and for many is an integral part of the healing process. Sharing the pain of your loss helps to make the load a little lighter. Sometimes, it's easier to say things in a private prayer than it is to another human. Learning to say what you need to through prayer may help you to say things you need or want to say to others in your life. Begin your prayer as you normally would depending on your tradition and whom you work with.

> *I reach out, to ease my pain.*
> *I reach out for comfort in my time of need.*
> *I reach out for strength.*
> *I feel loss. I feel pain. I feel grief.*
> *Help me to process through these emotions.*
> *Help me to heal.*

Take a moment to speak openly about your loss. Say whatever it is you need to get off your chest. We all have a multitude of feelings we encounter while experiencing loss. This can include anger. If you are mad, say so. Your anger is a legitimate feeling that can be safely expressed. When you are ready, continue:

*I know I will heal when the time comes.*
*I know I will carry on.*
*But now, I honor the loss,*
*I feel the pain.*
*I work through my grief.*
*Help me to process these emotions.*
*Help me to heal.*

Close your prayer as normal. You may feel the need to journal after this prayer or to curl up in a blanket. Both options are equally valid.

## Nightmare Sachet

Grief can utterly destabilize our entire life. When we grieve, that emotional pain has a physical effect on our bodies in addition to our mental health. It is not uncommon for grief to trigger nightmares and restless nights. Sleep is important for our body, mind, and spirit to rest, recuperate, and heal. This sachet is crafted with simple yet powerful ingredients that help comfort, provide peace, and ease those restless nights. Once the intentions are set to work, the sachet is kept under your pillow as you sleep. Let this working relieve your nighttime tension and allow you the rest that you need.

For this sachet you will need:

* A drawstring pouch, preferably white but black would work as well
* Garden sage
* Marjoram
* Lavender
* Chamomile
* Rose quartz

When you are ready, call upon any guides, deities, or spirits that you work with, or invoke your higher self. You may invite your guides to bless each ingredient as you focus on your intentions of relief, peace, and comfort.

Take the garden sage into the palm of your hand and call upon its intended purpose:

> *I bless this garden sage to cleanse my dreams and purify my spirit.*
> *Help me build emotional strength and heal my grief.*

Close your eyes and imagine a bright white light enveloping the sage as it is blessed and place it into the sachet. Take the marjoram next:

*I bless this marjoram to cleanse my mind and
bring happiness.*

*Help me relieve my grief and find joy again.*

Allow the bright white light to bless the marjoram and add
it to the sachet. Move on to the lavender:

*I bless this lavender to encourage mental wellness
and harmony.*

*Help me find peace and a restful sleep.*

Once the bright white light blesses the lavender, add it to
the sachet. Prepare the chamomile:

*I bless this chamomile to nurture tranquility and
healing.*

*Help me reduce stress.*

Add the chamomile to the sachet after it has been blessed
by the white light. Take the rose quartz crystal into your palm
and call on its energy:

*I bless this rose quartz to purify and open the heart.*

*Help me promote self-love, compassion, deep inner
healing, and feelings of peace.*

Bless the rose quartz with the bright white light and place
it into the sachet. Pull the drawstrings tight and tie them
together three times, binding the sachet. Hold it in your
hands, allowing everything to be blessed so that the energies

may work together for your purpose. When you are ready, remember to thank the guides that you have called on and leave the sachet under your pillow.

## Coping with Loneliness Spell

To cope with loneliness, it is important to understand it. Loneliness feels like a hole in your soul as isolation eats away at your self-esteem. It can be overwhelming and feels like a bottomless pit. So, how do we find peace? By filling the hole with things that make us feel loved. Finding peace in loneliness is a challenge, but nothing is impossible. Chronic loneliness is a deep yearning for understanding, acceptance, belonging. Finding these within yourself is the first step toward peace.

For this working you will need:

* A light blue or white candle

* Pen and paper

* Lavender essential oil or any lavender-infused oil

Begin by dressing the candle with the lavender essential oil or a lavender-infused oil while focusing on your intentions of finding peace and harmony. When you are ready, light the candle, speaking your intention out loud:

> *I seek peace within myself.*
> *I look inward to find harmony.*
> *I create a sense of belonging by belonging first to myself.*

After speaking your intention, grab the pen and paper. Create a list of three things that fill your soul, including hobbies such as dancing, cooking, or reading your favorite book. Think of things that help you feel more like yourself. Anything that you truly enjoy! Next, write three ways that you can reach out to others. You can join a book club, reconnect with friends on social media, sign up for volunteer work. Last, write down three positive affirmations that remind you to love yourself. You can use any of the affirmations listed earlier in this book or create custom affirmations that align with your intention.

Once your lists are ready, close your eyes. Reaffirm your intention as you imagine a bright light washing over you— whatever color feels most peaceful to you. Allow this light to cleanse you and be a source of comfort. This light is representative of your inner peace. Imagine this light filling the holes that you feel within your heart and soul, filling you with peace. Wrap your arms around yourself in a tight embrace. Be accepting and understanding of yourself and hold on to yourself until you are ready to release the energy.

After the working is complete, display your lists as a reminder to yourself. You can keep them on your altar or tape it to your bathroom mirror, anyplace that you will be able to refer back to it. This is your checklist. Repeat the affirmations to yourself as often as you need. Remember to do the activities that you love and bring you joy. Act on different ways to reach out to others. Your work in the mundane is just as important as your spiritual work; true growth requires both.

## Coping with Loneliness Meditations

This meditation is a form of self-reflection, taking a deep look within as you fill your soul. This is a shorter meditation that can be repeated as often as you need. As with all meditations in this book, take the time to prepare in advance. You can even take notes ahead of time to organize your thoughts and intentions. When you are ready, find a comfortable seat and close your eyes.

You find yourself in a garden. Look around, checking your surroundings. Notice the vegetation and the flowers. Listen to the sounds of the birds singing. Feel the wind blow through your hair. The sun is warm on your skin. What does your garden look like? How does your garden make you feel?

After you have explored the garden, you notice an empty garden planter off to the side. The planter is dirty, seemingly forgotten in the lush garden. Take some time here to clean the planter, revealing a beautiful pattern underneath. You find some fertile soil and some seeds or flowers. Take your time to fill the planter, providing the tender loving care it needs. The soil will nourish whatever you choose to plant here, allowing it to grow and thrive. Make sure to water and nurture the plant.

When you are ready, place the planter in the center of the garden. Watch as it grows and thrives until it is the strongest feature of your garden. Allow the roots to grow deep as the green leaves stretch toward the warm sun, full of life. This new plant attracts butterflies, birds, deer. The garden grows stronger and more beautiful than it was before.

Remember to return to your garden as often as you need. Allow this to be a place of comfort and solace. Most importantly, remember to nourish your soul as you nourish your garden so that you, too, may grow and thrive.

## Coping with Loneliness Affirmations

Human beings are social creatures. We tend to need interaction with others to help maintain healthy relationships. When those interactions are limited for whatever reason, it affects us, often negatively. Loneliness can result from different traumatic events, including the death of a loved one, or as we have recently seen, a worldwide pandemic. These affirmations are to help remind us of the positive as we work through feelings of seclusion.

* I am never truly alone. The [universe/my deity] is with me.
* I am my best source of comfort; I allow myself to receive it.
* I attract people who value me. I attract people I value.
* I find the quiet peace in solitude.
* I am my own best friend.
* All I need is in me.

Try combining affirmations together in different patterns and orders to create your own specialized wordings.

## Coping with Loneliness Prayer

When in need of divine compassion, our deities are only words away. Reach out to your higher power with your healing requests. As usual, open your prayer according to your pathway, and then continue:

> *When I'm lonely, I come to you*
> *In search of compassion and peace.*
> *While I understand I am enough,*
> *Isolation takes a toll.*
> *My heart aches for lost companionship.*
> *I pray for what I need to be brought into my life—*
> *To share a world of love*
> *To turn to when I am in need,*
> *To know I am not alone.*
> *Take my hand and guide me with love*
> *and compassion.*
> *Guide me to find contentment.*
> *Ease my loneliness and draw refuge to me.*
> *Fill me with hope and bless me with the comfort*
> *I seek.*

If you have a specific request or words of your own to say, do so now and then close your prayer as usual.

# Lavender Rose Hot Chocolate for Healing Heartache

They say that only time can mend a broken heart, but this lavender rose hot chocolate recipe is a bit of kitchen witchery to ease and heal an aching heart. Cacao has historically been used in Mayan and Aztec traditions to bring peace and open the heart. A mug of hot chocolate is the perfect comfort food to soothe heartache. For this recipe, we add rose buds for happiness and to nourish the heart, and lavender for peace, healing, and harmony.

For this recipe you will need:

* 1 cup of milk or nondairy milk alternative
* 1 tablespoon of organic food-grade rose buds or petals (any color)
* 1 teaspoon food-grade lavender buds
* ¼ teaspoon vanilla extract
* 2 tablespoons cacao powder (alternatively, cocoa powder can be used)
* Optional: 1 teaspoon honey

Take a moment to ground yourself before you begin, then set your intentions. Heat the milk or nondairy milk alternative on the stove with the rose and lavender, careful not to let it boil. Occasionally stir with a whisk, adding your own energy to work along with the flowers. Allow this to steep for 10 minutes. Turn off the heat and strain out the flowers.

Add the remaining ingredients and either use a frother or mix with a whisk.

Grab a cozy blanket and sit in your favorite comfortable chair. Close your eyes and take a sip, soothing your heart. Allow yourself to take this time to just simply *be*.

## Ritual for Rediscovering Yourself

Every day, we are changed. We are affected by the decisions we make and the experiences we live through, no matter how big or small they may appear to be. Whether it is recovering from a trauma, learning coping mechanisms, or just experiencing the chaos of our daily lives, we are impacted in profound ways. Sometimes, after all this change, we may no longer truly recognize who we are. This ritual will assist us in looking within to rediscover who we have become.

This ritual can be repeated as necessary or even combined with the Meditation for Rediscovering Yourself. Soul searching is a journey; take as much time as you need.

For this working you will need:

* A white or light blue candle
* A lighter or matches
* A mirror—any size will do
* A journal and something to write with
* Rose quartz
* Optional: rosemary incense

For this ritual you can sit in front of a mirror or use a smaller, handheld mirror. Any size is fine as long as you can see your entire face in the reflection. Begin this ritual by lighting the white or blue candle. You can call upon any guides or deities that you work with to assist you in this ritual.

Take the rose quartz in the palm of your dominant hand. If your mirror is a handheld one, take it in your nondominant hand. Set your intentions, and when you are ready, recite the following incantation:

> *Open my eyes so that I can see*
> *Who it is that I call me.*

Open your eyes. Hold the rose quartz to your heart and turn your gaze to the reflection in the mirror. The rose quartz is a stone for self-love and compassion. As you look upon yourself, take note of what you see, but do so with compassion for yourself. Focus first on your features—the line of your jaw, the angle of your nose, the fullness of your lips. Then turn to your eyes. Look beyond their shape and their color—look within yourself.

When you are ready to start writing, set the rose quartz down and pick up your journal and writing utensil. Return your gaze to your reflection and allow yourself to freewrite what—or rather, *who*—you see looking back at you. Allow the words to flow freely and remember to use compassion with yourself. Not only is this a self-discovery ritual, it is also a self-love ritual.

Take as much time as you need to write without over-thinking it. Let your thoughts go and just simply write. This allows our intuition to take over, opening the doors to the parts of ourselves that often remain hidden.

When you feel that you have expressed all that you can, let the pen fall. Pick the rose quartz up once more, returning it to your heart. Smile at your reflection with compassion and acceptance.

Thank your guides and keep the rose quartz on your altar to complete this ritual. Return to your journal and reflect on what you had written during the intuitive freewriting exercise. Self-discovery is a process; return to this journal and repeat this ritual as often as needed.

## Meditation for Rediscovering Yourself

Everything we experience in life—the ups and the downs—can impact who we are and how we see ourselves. Sometimes, we can lose sight of who we are. This meditation is designed for when you look in a mirror and no longer recognize the face looking back at you. The Meditation for Rediscovering Yourself can be practiced as often as needed and can be used with the Ritual for Rediscovering Yourself. Complete the tri-fecta by ending your practice with the affirmations included below this section.

This meditation is lengthy but simple in practice. To be fully prepared, I recommend reading through the medita-tion several times in advance. You can also choose to record yourself reading the meditation out loud to give you a guide to work with when you are ready to practice.

In this meditation, you will be meeting different versions of yourself—the "you" that you used to be, the "you" that has been burdened by chaos, and the "you" that you wish you could be. By meeting and morphing with each version of yourself, you are practicing self-acceptance, self-love, and self-discovery. You may want to have a journal and pen prepared for self-reflection after the practice. As always, set aside some uninterrupted time in a safe and comfortable space.

When you are ready to begin, close your eyes and allow yourself to be transported to a garden. Take a few moments here to explore the details of the garden around you. Notice the colors and fragrance of the flowers. Feel the breeze on your face. Touch the grass and note how it feels against your fingertips. Pay attention to what sounds you hear. Are there birds chirping? Can you hear a creek running? Are there any other animals around you? Take as much time as you need here; allow this to be a place of comfort, warmth, and security. You are safe here.

After you have explored your garden, imagine a path opens ahead of you. Take that first step forward in your journey and see where it takes you. Are you still in the garden? Anytime you feel distracted, return to the details of the path you are walking on.

Keep walking until you see someone ahead of you. As you come closer, you realize that this person is you—or rather, a version of you. Meet the "you" that you used to be before the chaos. Take a moment and just gaze upon this other you. As a past version of you, this figure may look younger, less bothered by the burdens that you have carried. Notice their features, their strengths, their weaknesses. Reach out and pull them in to a tight embrace. As you hug your other you, imagine that they are molding into you, becoming one with you. You may not see this version of yourself anymore, but they are a part of who you are within. Allow this version of you to be a source of comfort.

As you move forward, preparing to meet the next version of yourself, take a note of your surroundings, particularly if there are any changes in the scenery. Continue walking until you meet the "you" that has been burdened by chaos. Notice their features, their strengths, and their weaknesses. How do you feel seeing this version of you? Take note of any emotions or thoughts that come up here, then let them go. These feelings can be reflected on after the meditation is complete. When you are ready, reach forward to this other you and envelop them in a deep hug. Allow yourself to take them into you. Your burdens, trauma, and experiences are a part of you. Allow this version of you to be a source of strength.

Continue forward on your path. Return your attention to your surroundings. Remember that you are safe here. There is one more version of yourself for you to meet. When you are ready, welcome the "you" that you wish you could be. Notice their features, their strengths, their weaknesses. What do you feel when you see this version of you? Reach forward and take this version into you just as you have done with the others. The person that you wish to be is already a part of who you are. Allow this version of you to be a source of confidence.

Now that you have met and embraced these other versions of you, it is time to reach the final destination on this journey. Walk to the end of the path until you see a pool of clear water. This could be a pond or a well. Once you reach the water, look down to see your reflection. Now that you have embraced these other versions of you and accepted them as a part of you, what do you see when you look at your reflection? Take as much time as you need here. Notice your features, your strengths, and your weaknesses. See your comfort, your strength, and your confidence. Each of these versions of you are a part of your true self. When you put them all together, who are you?

When you are ready, open your eyes. Wrap your arms around yourself in a tight embrace. Hold yourself as long as you need. After you let go, turn to your journal. Reflect on your journey. Write down everything that you remember about the different versions of yourself that you met in the meditation. All these versions of yourself are just different aspects of who you are. By meeting each of them in the meditation, you rediscover who you are.

Take time to journal about what you experienced during this meditation.

## Affirmations for Rediscovering Yourself

Relearning who you are, changing who you are, deciding who you want to be—all are within the realm of possibility and an important part of your spiritual journey. Let these affirmations remind you of who you are each step of the way.

* I know who I am.
* I accept change from within.
* I live as my authentic self.
* I am who I am meant to be.
* I embrace every aspect of myself.
* My inner truth speaks, and I listen.
* I speak my truth and the world listens.
* My past changes me but does not define me.
* Every day I grow into the person I am meant to be.
* I am me.

As always, remember you can use each of these affirmations alone, or combine them together to create more complex groupings.

## A Prayer for Rediscovering Yourself

An important step to self-discovery is to always speak your truth. They say, "The truth will set you free," and that holds true here as well. Speaking your truth allows you to live and express yourself authentically, and this helps you to discover who you truly are. We are always changing, growing, and adapting to the world around us. As long as we continue to speak our truth, we will always know who we truly are. These prayers serve as a simple reminder as we call upon our guides, deities, or the universe to assist in the path to self-discovery.

Since the goal is to speak your truth, these prayers do not have to be followed exactly as written. If you feel the need to speak something out to the universe, trust that instinct. That is your inner truth waiting to be expressed. This script serves as a starting point to help inspire you. You are encouraged to always add your own personal touch and speak from the heart. Remember this from the affirmations for rediscovering yourself: I speak my truth and the world listens. The world is listening to your prayer, so go ahead and speak your truth.

When you are ready to begin, open your prayer in whatever way best suits your personal practice, and then continue:

> *Every day I change and grow,*
> *Every day I wonder.*
> *I find myself changed,*
> *And sometimes I don't recognize who I see.*
> *Assist me as I rediscover who I truly am.*
> *I am ready to speak my truth,*
> *Please, let the world listen.*

During this prayer, you may find different thoughts or feelings popping into your head. Make note of these to journal about and reflect on—these are a part of your inner truth. Self-discovery is often intuitive. Revelations can happen when we let go of control and trust our instincts.

Magical self-care has really made a major impact on wellness and how we deal with all that we experience in life. These practices have brought us many new tools to assist in coping with the challenges and struggles we face every day. Working with these practices helps us with inner healing, developing healthy coping mechanisms, and discovering new things about ourselves, all of which prepares us for the next chapter of this book: shadow work.

# 8

## Shadow Work

**W**here there is light, there must also be darkness. Like night and day, the yin and yang. The two naturally go together as counterparts. Where one is expected, the other will follow. Even the brightest room can disguise nooks and crannies where darkness lies hidden. We all have our own nooks and crannies where darkness lies hidden too. These dark aspects to our personalities may be things we don't always show or may not even be aware we have. These dark aspects combined are known as your shadow self.

Essentially, the shadow is the parts of you that you don't always see, as they are often buried beneath the surface. These are the emotions that we try to stuff down because we view them as negative or inferior: rage, jealousy, regret, greed, self-ishness, desire for power, etc. Since we view these things as negative, we cut ourselves off from them, effectively burying parts of our personality. This dissociation creates a split deep within us, leaving a part of us fragmented and forgotten.

The shadow cannot be eliminated, only repressed. Every time a feeling is repressed, the shadow grows. Repression can be dangerous, as some things can only be buried so deep. The shadow self can easily be triggered, leading to involuntary outbursts of anger or other actions that leave you feeling quite unlike your "normal" self.

The shadow is not only made of negative traits. There are many times when positive aspects of our personalities—such as strength and confidence—are suppressed. When we are silenced, our accomplishments ridiculed, or deemed to be "too much" by others, we suppress amazing parts of ourselves to suit others. By doing so, we continue to feed our shadow. The shadow self must be addressed and faced to move forward in your journey. This brings us to shadow work.

Shadow work is a form of psychoanalysis pioneered by twentieth-century Swiss psychologist Carl Jung. He believed that true balance and harmony could only be achieved by decompartmentalizing these repressed aspects of ourselves and reintegrating them with the rest of our personalities. Jung addressed the shadow within himself in his book *Modern Man in Search of a Soul*, saying, "How can I be substantial if I do not cast a shadow? I must have a dark side also if I am to be whole."[2]

---

2. Carl G. Jung, *Modern Man in Search of a Soul* (London: Routledge and Kegan Paul, 1933), 35.

Taking care of yourself requires treating your shadow self. Light and love is only one side of the coin. You must acknowledge your shadow, understand it, and learn from it to truly heal. The shadow is not something to fear, nor is it something to feel shame over. As Jung says in *Psychology and Alchemy*, "There is no light without shadow and no psychic wholeness without imperfection."[3] By embracing our imperfections, we can find peace.

## Approaching Shadow Work

There are many ways to approach shadow work. Working with a licensed professional therapist is highly encouraged, especially if there is any unresolved trauma. It is also recommended to have developed healthy coping mechanisms in place for when preparing to meet your shadow.

Journaling, creative works, meditation, and spellwork can all be used in shadow work, in addition to therapy. When it comes to shadow work, use the methods that work best for you and your own personal practice.

Before you begin shadow work, there are a few tips to help ensure a more beneficial experience:

* Release self-judgment. Shadow work requires you to be vulnerable with yourself.

---

3. Carl G. Jung, *Psychology and Alchemy* (London: Routledge and Kegan Paul, 1953), 152.

Treat yourself with compassion and kindness, or else you will only continue to feed your shadow.

* Ask why. To get to the root of these new emotions, it is important to ask *why* you are feeling a particular way. Addressing why you feel a certain way will help you discover where the feeling came from so that you can heal from it.

* Be honest. Honesty is the best policy, and it is a major component of shadow work. If you cannot be truly honest with yourself, you will not be able to move forward.

* Take your time. You cannot process everything all at once. Take your time. Shadow work does not need to be done daily. In fact, it shouldn't be. There are no deadlines, so there is no reason to rush. Take as much time as you need to process, heal, and recover before moving forward. Have patience with yourself.

* Be prepared. When it is time to address your shadow, make sure you are in a comfortable and safe space where you will not be interrupted. It is important to be centered and focused. Have a journal ready to record your thoughts and experiences. A glass of water or a box of tissues may be helpful as well.

* Aftercare. After doing any shadow work, it is important that you take the time to ground yourself. Allow yourself to come back to the present moment and spend some time taking care of yourself. Self-love and self-acceptance are the root of shadow work.

## Tools for Shadow Work

When doing shadow work, there are many magical tools that can assist you in your practice: herbs, stones and crystals, a journal for recording thoughts and experiences, or a mirror for self-reflection.

Shadow work herbs can be burned as incense, left as offerings, or sealed in a sachet or spell jar. Additionally, they can be used in the form of essential oils, which can be diffused in an aromatherapy diffuser or diluted with a carrier oil and applied topically. Here are our favorite herbs for assisting with shadow work and their metaphysical properties:

* Garden sage promotes clarity and spiritual wisdom and cleanses negativity and fear.

* Rosemary enhances memory and concentration.

* Lavender relieves stress by fostering peace and harmony, which improves mental wellness and allows for a restful sleep.

* Chamomile promotes tranquility and relieves stress by soothing tension.

* Eucalyptus is used for cleansing, healing, and warding for protection before, during, and after shadow work.

* Lemongrass is uplifting and revitalizing, and it is useful in recovery after shadow work.

Stones and crystals are useful tools for shadow work as well as the recovery process. They can be placed on the body or held during meditation or placed in front of or around you. Here are our favorite stones and crystals for assisting with shadow work and their metaphysical properties:

* Black obsidian helps us to see our shadows and promotes healing by helping to dissolve blockages that could be holding us back. It reveals our inner truth by acting as a mirror to the soul.

* Snowflake obsidian works very similarly to black obsidian regarding revealing our shadow self and helps us to attain freedom as we break the chains holding us down. The black and white design promotes balance between light and dark.

* Labradorite can be used to stimulate forgotten memories and breaks down illusions. As it strengthens intuition, we can look deeper within ourselves to seek the truth. Labradorite is great for revealing hidden patterns for self-reflection.

* Lapis lazuli encourages self-awareness and self-expression, and it helps with facing the truth. This stone is used to promote wisdom, balance, and emotional healing.

* Sodalite is known as "the truth stone" and encourages self-acceptance by helping to release self-judgment as we reveal the suppressed parts of our personalities.

* Black tourmaline is a protection stone used for deep grounding. It encourages objective and logical thought processes while relieving tension and dispelling fear and anger.

* Selenite is used for cleansing and protection. It promotes reconnection between your two selves and cleanses negativity. Selenite pairs nicely with black tourmaline.

* Amethyst bestows spiritual wakefulness by connecting the mind, body, and spirit. This is a great stone for meditation, as it encourages inner peace and helps to quiet the mind. Amethyst is also used as support for overcoming grief and loss.

* Rose quartz ignites self-love and compassion and helps improve self-esteem and body image. This helps us alleviate our worries and negative thoughts and feelings to help heal the heart.

Journaling is an important part of shadow work. It allows us to use our voice and fully express our thoughts and feelings. Recording our shadow work sessions also allows us to more easily evaluate hidden patterns that may have been missed otherwise. There are many shadow work prompts for journaling exercises. Even when doing shadow work through spells, rituals, and meditations, having a written account afterward may be beneficial to your practice.

A mirror is also a great tool for shadow work, as the eyes are the windows to the soul. Sometimes to look within, we need to literally look at ourselves. When using a mirror in shadow work, it is important to practice non-judgment. To heal the shadow self, we must be fully accepting of all aspects of who we are. Non-judgment can be challenging, but it is vital.

Although shadow work is extremely important for your spiritual journey and will in fact be a great deal of your travels, it must be emphasized this type of work is not to be entered into lightly. Encountering the shadow without proper coping skills can be detrimental. That being said, if you are serious and attentive to yourself, you will know when you are ready to meet your darker side. If you do not feel ready, you are not ready. It is that simple. Do not let anyone push you into work you are not ready for. Social media is filled with misinformation. I can't tell you how many times I have seen posts in groups or videos of people pushing others into shadow work using intimidation. This is a red flag—if someone is using intimidation to push shadow work, don't listen to them. Threats of "You will never get anywhere without it" are meant to scare you and get them views. Shadow work is an incredibly personal journey. No one can tell you when you are equipped for the journey better than you can. No one can take your journey for you. It is for you and you alone.

Because shadow work involves revealing the hidden, this means revisiting past traumas. It can also mean remembering or recognizing past traumas for the first time. This can be deeply painful work. Be ready for it.

Shadow work takes preparation. The rest of this chapter includes spells, rituals, meditations, and journaling prompts for when you are ready to begin.

## Cord Cutting Ritual

A cord cutting ritual is a powerful tool for energetically cutting ties to other people, unpleasant situations, or even to negative traits within ourselves. This helps to finalize severing physical and mental connections in the mundane world and is a great way to enter the realm of shadow work. As we cut ties with negative or toxic things around us, we can begin to look inward and reflect on ourselves.

For this working you will need:

* Two taper or chime candles, preferably white or one white and one black
* A safety pin

* A flammable cord or string, about nine inches long
* A lighter
* Firesafe plate or tray
* White salt
* Journal and pen

Before beginning this ritual, the candles will need to be prepared. Using the safety pin, you will carve your name longways down the side of the first candle. If using two different colored candles, the white one will be the first candle. For the second candle, or the black candle, you will carve the name of whomever—or whatever—it is that you are looking to cut ties with. Once the candles are prepared, take the cord or string and wrap it around the first candle three times. Leave some slack, and wrap the other end around the second candle, also three times. Each candle will be wrapped by the connecting cord as a representation of the energetic connection.

Place the connected candles on a firesafe plate or tray and encircle them with a ring of white salt. Be sure that the ring of salt is large enough that both candles fit inside. The circle does not have to be perfect, but try to make it as even as you can.

When you are ready, call upon any higher power or spirit guides to assist you in this working and set your intention. Focus on each candle for a moment, close your eyes, and see in your mind what each candle represents to you. After your intentions are set, light the wick of each candle, starting with your candle. You can speak your intentions out loud; ask for the energetic connections to be severed as the cord burns away, or sit in quiet reflection.

As the candles burn down, the cord will eventually catch fire and burn away. (Keep a close eye on the cord and flame to ensure your safety. Do not leave this ritual unattended for any reason.) Allow the cord and both the candles to burn out completely before ending your working. Follow up with your journal, reflecting on these questions and anything else you wish to record:

* What steps did you take to sever this connection in the mundane world?
* What will you do to ensure this connection remains severed?
* What did you feel in your body as the cords were severed?
* What does severing this connection mean to you?
* What aspects of your shadow were revealed to you while completing this ritual?
* How will you heal and care for yourself moving forward?

# Cord Cutting Meditation

If the required materials for the cord cutting ritual are not available to you, it is possible to cut energetic ties through meditation instead of spellwork. Cord cutting meditations are just as effective and are a firesafe option. This meditation can be completed in addition to the ritual or repeated on your own as often as you desire. The cord cutting meditation is very simple in nature and easily customizable to best suit your needs.

When you are ready to begin, close your eyes and center yourself, and align with your intention. See yourself sitting in a comfortable room. Have a look around and notice the subtle details around you. Know that you are safe here in this space. Look across from you. On the other side of the room, you see the person or situation that you are connected to. Take your time, see the details. If this is a person, imagine their face, their clothes, their voice. Notice what they are doing. If the connection is a situation, allow yourself to see the scene play over and over. Whatever it is that you want to cut ties with, focus on the details to see it very clearly on the other side of the room.

However, please note that for some events or people, you may not want to see their face or don't care to repeat the event in your mind even once, and definitely not over and over. This is completely understandable. In these situations, I prefer to visualize the offender as a black void. A blank space that I can shrink down to whatever size I wish. Remember, you can use symbolic representations when you want to.

Once you have a clear picture or a void in mind, imagine a large, thick, black rope wrapping around your waist. The rope crosses the room and continues to wrap its way around on the other side. For a moment, you are trapped, tied to the other side.

Take a pair of large scissors in your hand and begin to cut away at the black cord. See the cord fall away and the wrapping drop. You are free. The other side of the room begins to fall away; the connection has been severed. See yourself as you wish to be without this connection holding you back and return from your meditative state.

## Letter to Your Shadow Self

Writing is a cathartic practice that helps unleash hidden emotions as we express the deepest parts of ourselves. This practice is a form of shadow work that can be repeated often and customized to suit your specific needs and desires. The concept is simple—we are writing letters to our shadow selves in a safe and comfortable environment. There is no right or wrong way to conduct this freewriting exercise as long as you are authentic, honest, and free of self-judgments. The first step is to ensure that you are comfortable and have a stretch of uninterrupted alone time—we can more easily and more honestly connect with our shadow selves when we are alone. It is easier to let go of judgments when we do not feel any outside pressure.

For this working you will need:

* Pen and paper
* Optional: a lighter or match and a firesafe container
* Optional: a shovel and pot of soil or space of earth outdoors

You can write as many letters as you choose but allow each letter to focus on just one aspect of your shadow self. As you write, explore the specific trait that you are choosing to focus on. Speak to this part of you. Discover where this shadow came from; what act of suppression caused you to repress this part of you? How can you unbury it and release it? How can you heal this part of you, connect with it, and move forward? Do not hold back any emotions; write everything, even the things that may be hard for you to admit to yourself.

Freewriting allows us to express the parts of ourselves that we keep hidden. Self-expression helps to unbury the shadow. Practicing non-judgment and forgiveness heals the shadow. Processing and moving forward allows you to integrate the shadow in a healthy and positive manner.

After you have finished writing, take the time to read through the whole letter. Sometimes the words may surprise you. Notice how these words make you feel. Use this as the chance to truly get to know your shadow. When you are ready, there are a couple of options available for the next step.

The letter can either be burned in a firesafe container or it can be buried in the earth, where it will eventually break down. Either method can be used to release the shadow.

Whichever option you choose to release the letter, take a moment of silence afterward. Turn your attention inward. Pay attention to any areas that feel heavy. Send love, healing, and forgiveness to these areas. Wrap your arms around yourself in a tight embrace. Stay here as long as you need. Self-love is vital to shadow work.

## Out with the Old and In with the New Ritual

This is a two-part ritual designed for letting go of negative behaviors and old patterns while paving the way for a stronger and more empowered you. It's time to dive deep and dust the cobwebs off the dark corners of your soul to reflect on the parts of yourself that you keep hidden. With this working, you can embody the traits and qualities that you desire to create a profound transformation.

For this ritual you will need to create two custom herbal mixes, one for banishing and one for empowerment. There are numerous herbs for these purposes; build your blend based on what is available to you. Some recommended herbs for a banishing mix are nettle, agrimony, black pepper, mullein, juniper berries, and onion powder or dried minced onion. For the empowerment blend, you can use any mix of the following herbs: celandine, chili pepper, cinnamon, fennel, sandalwood, blessed thistle, cedar, or motherwort.

For this working you will need:

* A white candle
* A firesafe container
* A charcoal tablet
* A lighter
* Pen and 2 pieces of paper
* Banishing herb mix
* Empowerment herb mix
* A spoon or scoop

Ground and center yourself and prepare the charcoal tablet. If you work with any guides or deities, feel free to call upon them for their assistance and to watch over you during this ritual. When you are ready, light the white candle and speak your intention:

> *I come to let go and release so that I may step forth with renewed strength, clarity, and empowerment.*

Take the first piece of paper. Reflect on negative behaviors, old patterns, self-doubt, and anything that holds you back. Begin to write "I let go of…" and list each quality, one at a time. You can write as little or as much as you want. Feel free to be as descriptive as you like and hold nothing back.

Once you are ready, fold the paper three times away from you to banish these behaviors. Light the corner of the paper with the flame of the white candle and drop it into the firesafe container, saying:

*I release that which no longer serves me.*
*As is my will, so mote it be.*

As the paper burns, carefully scoop the banishing herb mix into the fire. Focus on your intention; allow these behaviors, thoughts, patterns, and attitudes to leave you. When the paper has burned and the flame dies down, move on to the second piece of paper.

On the second piece of paper, write down intentions that empower you. Write what you want to attract, list the attitudes and behaviors you want to develop, and include the new patterns you would like to build. Be as detailed as you like. At the end of the list, write "I am empowered to be who I am." Fold the paper three times, this time toward you to attract these things to you. Once again, light the corner of the paper with the flame of the white candle and drop it into the firesafe container, saying:

*I attract only that which will serve me.*
*As is my will, so mote it be.*

As the paper burns, safely scoop the empowerment herb mix into the fire. Focus on your intention; see yourself building new patterns, transforming into a more empowered you. When the embers have fully burned and it is safe to move them, scatter the ashes to the wind, finalizing your intention with these words:

> *I arise from the ashes anew, renewed, and empowered.*
> *As is my will, so mote it be.*

## Healing Your Inner Child Meditation

Healing your inner child is an extremely important step within shadow work. When we are young, we often suppress many things to seek approval and praise from our peers as well as from the adults in our life. As we grow older, these aspects of ourselves that we spent so many years suppressing build up in our shadow selves. As we work to understand and positively integrate our shadow selves, our inner child is left vulnerable. Through this meditation, we will connect with our inner child and provide them with the love and care they need to heal. This meditation can be repeated as needed, but it is reserved to be one of the final shadow work activities in this book. As always, prepare your meditation in advance and ensure you have a comfortable space where you will not be interrupted.

As we begin this meditation and set our intentions, let us close our eyes and imagine ourselves in a peaceful garden. This may be the same meditative garden that we have worked with in past meditations, or you can imagine an entirely new garden. Wherever you are, take a moment to notice the sights around you. Smell the flora, hear the birds sing, feel the grass beneath your feet.

After you familiarize yourself with your garden, look ahead of you to find your inner child. Your inner child often resembles a version of you when you were younger. Notice what your inner child is doing. Are they enjoying a picnic? Playing in the sand? Swinging on a swing set or coloring a picture? What activity are they engaging in, and what emotions do they seem to be feeling? What does their area of the garden look like? In what ways is it like the rest of the garden? In what ways is it different?

When you are ready, join your inner child in their area of the garden. If they are coloring, you can color too. If they are swinging on a swing set, give them a gentle push from behind. Take some time simply being with your inner child. Give them the attention that they deserve from you. As you spend time together, feel free to open a dialogue with your inner child. You can ask what it is they need, what they want to do, and how they feel. Truly listen and communicate with your inner child and be sure to follow through with what you say. Let your inner child feel heard and show them that they are loved and appreciated. Give them the care that you needed as a child and love them in the way that you needed to be loved. Allow them to be a child just doing the things that kids like to do—the things that we no longer do now as adults. Most importantly, allow them to be their authentic selves with no pressure to suppress any part of themselves.

Spend as much time as you need with your inner child, showing them love and encouraging them to be their authentic self. When you are ready, be sure to wrap your arms around your inner child and hold them in a tight embrace before leaving your garden. As you return to the present moment, wrap your arms around yourself and hold yourself in a tight embrace, just as you did with your inner child in the meditation. Know that your inner child is still a part of you that deserves love and care. Self-love and self-care include loving and caring for your inner child instead of suppressing them in favor of adulthood.

## Aftercare and Recovery

Shadow work can be a physically, mentally, and even emotionally draining process. It is normal to feel exhausted after practicing shadow work. Aftercare is vital for a healthy recovery. There are many ways to practice aftercare to recover from shadow work: drinking plenty of water, eating a grounding meal, or taking a relaxing bath with bath salts are just a few examples. An effective aftercare process needs to ground our energy, nourish our body, and comfort us with self-love and self-care.

## HYDRATING MOON WATER

Moon water is a common tool used in many witchcraft practices for spellwork and manifestation due to its concentration of lunar energy and properties of spiritual transformation and blessing. Moon water can also be used to hydrate and bless the body when recovering after shadow work. This is one of the simplest recipes in this book, but it is filled with intention and power.

For this recipe you will need:

* At least 16 ounces of drinkable water in a closed, transparent container or bottle
* Access to the full moon

After the full moon has risen, simply place your container or bottle of water under the moonlight and set your intentions. You can place crystals or herbs around the water (but not in it; water is bad for some stones and crystals), ask for blessings from your guides or deities, or recite an incantation or affirmation. The water can be left on a windowsill or outside, whatever is accessible and preferable to you. It does not need to charge all night, even just two hours is fine. Direct access to moonlight is not necessary, so don't worry if the skies are overcast.

When to bring in your moon-charged water depends upon your personal practice. Some practices focus more on the intention, so it is okay if the water is not brought in until after the sun has risen. Other practices hold the belief that moon water should never touch the light of day. This is entirely up to you, so do what works best for your own practice.

Drinking this water after a shadow work practice will provide an extra energetic boost to cleanse, refresh, and bless your mind and spirit while hydrating your body.

## NOURISHING NETTLE INFUSION

Stinging nettle is used in metaphysical and magical practices for protection and to assist in blocking negativity. Additionally, culinary-grade dried stinging nettle leaf can be used to create a nourishing herbal tonic that is high in vitamin K and fuels the body with trace minerals and antioxidants. For an additional magical boost, you can use moon water.

Herbal infusions are different from your standard cup of tea. Herbal teas use a small amount of herbs that are steeped for only about 3–5 minutes. An herbal infusion is a tonic consisting of a larger amount of herbs steeped for a minimum of 4 hours and for up to 24 hours.

For this recipe you will need:

* 16 ounces of boiling water in a pot with a lid
* 4 ounces of sifted or cut culinary-grade dried stinging nettle
* A pitcher or 1-pint mason jar with lid
* A cheesecloth or large tea strainer
* Sweetener of choice for taste

Once the water starts to boil, turn the stove off and remove the pot from the heat. Add the stinging nettle, place the lid on top of the pot, and allow the mixture to infuse for at least 4 hours. If you intend to allow the infusion to steep for longer than 4 hours, you may want to move it to the refrigerator so that it lasts longer. Strain the mixture and dispose of the herbs when transferring to a pitcher or a mason jar, and then the infusion is ready to drink. The infusion will last up to 3 days in the refrigerator.

The stinging nettle infusion has a very earthy taste. This flavor is great for grounding but may be bitter on its own. Add your favorite sweetener for taste—honey, sugar, maple syrup, or agave nectar are popular choices. You can also use your moon water to make this infusion.

### GROUNDING CHEESE BOARD

It is important to ground after workings that use our energy, and shadow work is no exception. Food is a great way to fuel our body while providing a comforting and grounding experience. A French-inspired cheese board is easily customizable for dietary needs and preferences (there are even many vegan cheeses available).

For this recipe you will need:

* At least 3 kinds of cheese or nondairy cheese alternative
* Fresh or dried fruit

* Sliced Vienna bread, crostini, or crackers

* A selection of your favorite nuts and seeds

* A piece of your favorite chocolate or candy

* Optional: Sliced meats such as salami, prosciutto, or pepperoni

* A wooden board or platter large enough to fit your selection

There is no wrong way to lay out a cheese board. Feel free to include as many or as few options as you like. Cheese boards are great for experimenting, so add something new that you have always wanted to try! You can keep it simple with a few of your favorites or create a complex masterpiece combining new and bold flavors.

Your cheese board can be prepared in advance before your shadow work session, just leave it in the refrigerator until you are ready. When putting your cheese board together, you may want to use one of the food prep blessings provided earlier in this book. Allow the cheese board to be a spiritual experience.

## Cleansing Aftercare Meditation with Purification Bath Salts

As we know, the bathtub is a perfect location for cleansing not just physically but mentally, emotionally, and spiritually as well. This cleansing aftercare meditation with purification bath salts provides a magical meditative experience to help wash away the heaviness felt after shadow work. This meditation is a ritualistic experience in itself.

You may create a spa-like ambience by lighting white candles or playing some quiet, relaxing music—whatever will help you feel relaxed and comfortable.

### PURIFICATION BATH SALTS

Adding these bath salts to any bath will cleanse and purify the mind and spirit as you cleanse your body.

For these bath salts you will need:

* 1 cup of any combination of bath salts: Epsom salts, sea salt, pink Himalayan salt
* ½ tablespoon blessed thistle
* ½ tablespoon hyssop
* ½ tablespoon culinary sage
* ½ tablespoon rosemary
* ½ tablespoon peppermint
* A bowl and spoon or spatula for mixing
* Any 8 ounce jar with a lid
* Optional: colloidal oatmeal for baths

Combine all the ingredients in a bowl and mix until well combined, then transfer into a jar that has a lid. Depending on how much you choose to use, this mixture should last 4–8 baths.

## CLEANSING AFTERCARE MEDITATION

For this meditative practice, prepare the bathwater with the bath salts before you step in. When you are ready, use your hand or even a large kitchen spoon to sir the bathwater counterclockwise three times as you set your intention and recite the following:

> *I banish negative energy from myself and this space.*
>
> *I release that which does not serve me.*

Now stir the bath water clockwise three times and say:

> *I am cleansed as this space is cleansed.*
>
> *I purify my body, my mind, and my spirit.*

Enter the bathtub, taking a moment to get settled and comfortable. Close your eyes and take ten slow, deep breaths. With each inhale, imagine a bright, white light filling your body from top to bottom. With the exhale, release and allow the light to wash away any negativity you feel. Pay special attention to any areas that feel especially heavy or dark and send extra purifying energy there. If you feel ten breaths is not enough, take as much time as you need.

After energetically cleansing with the bright, white light, open your eyes so that you can safely move into a standing position. When you are ready, get your washcloth or loofah—whatever you use when bathing. This time, starting from the bottom of your feet and slowly working upward, physically cleanse every part of your body, washing three times counterclockwise, then three times clockwise again. If you choose, you can repeat the same incantations used to bless the bathwater.

Continue moving this way until you get to the top of your head. Close your eyes and squeeze the water out over your head, allowing the water to drip down your body before ending your bath.

Shadow work is a deeply personal practice that can look different for everyone. There are no timelines when it comes to shadow work. Some start shadow work early in their practice, while others may wait until they are deep in their practice before connecting with their shadow side. The most important facet of shadow work is doing what is best for you and your own practice. What works for some may not work for others. Take what works for you and leave the rest. A strong shadow work practice is dependent upon stability. If at any time a shadow work ritual, meditation, or activity triggers a negative experience, brings up unresolved trauma, or uncovers a new hidden trauma, it is important to seek professional help. After all, shadow work comes from therapy, and sometimes we must return to that foundation before moving forward.

# 9
## Healing Others

We live, play, and work in many different types of societies, and many different types of societies can mean many different issues that may need healing. From smaller localized societies, such as your coven, to larger, broader societies, such as your country and the world, we have learned healing needs to take place everywhere. Healing is what allows us to move forward and evolve to a higher level. In this final chapter, we will share spells and rituals to heal a variety of social issues.

When appropriate, these rituals can be adjusted for group use. When we perform ritual in a group, the multiple energies feed off each other, allowing for a greater energy buildup and shifting. Group work multiplies power and energy exponentially.

# Ritual to Heal Your Family

Some family traumas can be worked through, keeping a family intact. Others, not so much. It is important to point out healing your family is not the same thing as bringing your family together in agreement. Healing does not necessarily mean a family will be brought back together, nor stay in place. It means each person in the family deserves healing. Healing may include physical distance, emotional distance, or both between the members. This ritual is to heal each of the people involved, not bend them to a will they do not wish to be bent to.

If possible, the family should perform this ritual together. If not, it is okay. You can send out healing energies to any family members who are unable to be present but are willing to work the ritual with you. Family members who do not want to be included, or who do not know this is happening, should not be included. Respecting wishes may bring additional healing at a later time.

Each person will need to prepare a letter ahead of time. Family members who are not physically present may send in a letter. This letter should be sealed in an envelope and not read by anyone. In your letter, write out a list of your grievances with your family members. What do you feel was done against you? How do you feel you were harmed? No one else will see your letter, so write freely from the heart. Whether you have discussed these matters with the involved family members or not, write it all down. Getting it down onto paper is a way to physically remove these issues from your body. Let them go as the ink flows across the paper. Release any pain, anxiety, or other negative feelings these grievances bring up in you. We are not "forgiving and forgetting" in this letter; your intention is to remove some of the built-up, pent-up negative energy these issues have brought with them. Removing this negative energy is neccssary for each individual member of the family to heal. It is necessary for each individual to heal in order for the family to heal. If you feel your brother was an asshole, say so, but also say why. What actions were done (or not done) that affected your feelings? You can give specifics or just generalizations, such as physically or mentally abusive. Again, as you write, you want to focus on pulling negative energy out and pushing it into the paper. Seal it into an envelope when you are done.

For the rest of this ritual, you will need:

* A safe way to burn. This may mean an indoor fireplace, an outdoor bonfire, or the inside of a cauldron or other fireproof container. Because of the amount of paper you will be burning, this needs to be done outside if you are not using an indoor fireplace. Otherwise, you run the risk of setting off smoke detectors.

* Matches or lighter if necessary.

* A brown chime or taper candle for each participant, along with a safe way to hold them to

protect from hot dripping wax. We use brown as it not only symbolizes family issues, it also corresponds with decision-making (we are making a decision to let go of negativity), grace, and strength. It is also a color for grounding and neutrality. These correspond with ridding our systems of negative energy.

* The following dried herbs:
  - Angelica
  - Balm of Gilead
  - Dandelion
  - Horehound
  - Nettle
  - Pine needles
  - Ribbon strips of birch bark

How much of these you need will depend on how many people will be taking part in the ritual. You will combine all these ingredients together to form an incense. Each participant should have about 2 tablespoons. You can either give each person a small bowl with theirs in it or have everyone take from one community bowl during the ritual. Just make sure there is enough to go around for everyone.

If everyone is willing, you can mix the herbs into the incense together, taking turns adding ingredients and, if available, using a mortar and pestle to grind them finer. As the ingredients are combined, everyone's intention should be on creating an incense that will help to release negative energies.

When you are ready to perform the ritual, everyone should take up a position around the fire or fireproof container. If you are inside with a fireplace, spread out in front of it.

If your family is comfortable with it, hold hands.

Everyone say together:

*We come together, to help one another heal.*
*We are of the same blood but are not of the*
*same mind.*
*Our past together has caused pain.*
*As a family, we release the pain.*
*We wish healing for ourselves.*
*We wish healing for each other.*

If you held hands, you may drop them now. Each person should light their brown candle.

Take turns according to birth date, not age. In the case of multiple births on the same day, break it down by time of birth. The person whose birthday is closest to January 1 goes first, moving progressively through the year. Hold the lit candle in your dominant (or power) hand and the letter in the other. Say:

*I release that which does not serve me.*
*I set this energy free.*

Light the envelope with the brown candle and toss it either into the fire or the fireproof container you are using. Be sure to light the envelope with the brown candle before throwing it into the fire. You want to ensure you are the connective reason the energy goes up in cleansing flames. Follow up with the incense. If you are using a bonfire or fireplace, toss your incense into the flames. If you are using a fireproof container, very gently and carefully sprinkle bits of the incense on your envelope as it burns. It will be more difficult to burn in a container, so carefully relight the papers with your candle if necessary. Visualize the cleansing of the energy as you watch your offering burn. Your turn does not end until your papers are completely burned. Once they have, extinguish your candle.

Allow each person their moment. It is imperative everyone remain respectful and silent for each other, holding space. If there are people not present but their letters are, someone should light the envelope and complete the process for them.

When everyone is finished, you may hold hands again if you wish. Continue:

*We release this energy through cleansing fire.*
*Healing thoughts we do inspire.*

Depending on the dynamics in your family, you may want to end this ritual right away and go your separate ways. Or you may want to stand around the fire for a while, soaking in the warming energy of the flames. Either response is acceptable.

## Coven Closure

In a perfect scenario, when a person leaves a coven they have been initiated into, there is a ritual to release the person from both their oath and their energetic connection to the rest of the group. Sadly, there aren't always perfect scenarios.

It's happened to me. Maybe it's happened to you. The coven that you swore an oath to, and they swore an oath to you, implodes when the oath is broken. It can destroy the coven and leave the members in need of healing. In these situations, it seldom ends with closure, so healing is incomplete. Feelings of betrayal, disappointment, and disconnection have not been addressed. There is also the issue of the energy disruption created when people who are bound together are suddenly not on the same page. Anger, hurt, and resentment from one can still be felt by others since the energetic connection previously created has not been properly severed.

Without severing those ties, you may feel like you are the victim of a psychic vampire (or several), because basically you are. A broken oath may sever the bond, but it does not sever the energetic connection that remains. You have every right and reason to perform this ritual to fully sever the oath bond and allow yourself to heal.

For this ritual you will need:

* 1 black chime candle to represent each person in your coven including yourself (6 people—

6 candles). Each candle needs to be inscribed with the name of the person it represents.

* Sand
* A tray or plate big enough to hold the chime candles in a circle
* Thin hemp twine (in black if you can find it)
* A fireproof container such as a small cauldron
* Self-lighting charcoal tablet
* A pinch each of:
  - Frankincense resin
  - Myrrh resin
  - Lavender buds
* A few drops of lemon and orange essential oils
* A lighter

Set up your altar as normal, leaving a large space in the center to incorporate the materials for this working. The empty space will need to be able to fit your tray or plate and your fireproof container or cauldron.

Pour the sand onto the plate to create a firesafe area in which to perform this unbinding ritual.

Place the candle representing you in the very center of the plate and arrange the rest of the candles in a circle around you, the centerpiece. Place the plate on the altar with the fireproof container directly in front of it with the charcoal tablet inside. Place the rest of your supplies nearby or on your altar if it is large enough to hold everything. Light the charcoal tablet when you are ready to begin.

While the charcoal tablet is lighting itself, open your ritual as you normally would by calling to the elements, your deity (or deities), etc.

Begin by taking the center candle, which represents you, and tie the hemp twine to it about halfway down. Place the candle back in the center of your altar. Starting with the candle in the outer circle that is the farthest away from you (so behind your candle somewhere) run the twine to it, wrap it around the candle, and then back to your own. Move to the next candle going clockwise, run the twine to it, wrap it around the candle, and then wrap it back around your own again. Continue doing this moving clockwise around the circle, wrapping the twine from each candle back to you and then on to the next candle. After reaching the last candle, bring it back to you one more time, trim the hemp, and tie the end to your candle.

Sprinkle the frankincense onto the charcoal tablet and say:

*An oath was made,*
*An oath was not kept.*

Light the first candle you wrapped after your own and say:

*I release you [name of the person the candle represents],*

*An oath was made,*

*An oath was not kept.*

*You are released from your bond to me.*

*I am released from my bond to you.*

Continue around the circle, lighting each candle as you go and repeating the above.

When only your candle remains, light it and say:

*An oath was made,*

*An oath was not kept.*

*You are all released from your bond to me.*

*I am released from my bond to all of you.*

Add the myrrh to the charcoal tablet and take a seat to get comfortable while you watch and wait for the twine to burn away. Be sure to keep a close eye on it to make sure no part of the flames gets out of control, but also to help visualize the burning away of the bond that is being released.

Call your energy back to you from each person whose name is written on a candle around yours. Call out to them in your mind and tell each one:

*I sever our connection and reclaim my energy.*

Visualize this concept in your mind in a way that works for you—see your energetic connection with the other person cut off. The flow of energy between the two of you stopped. Any energy that is yours returns to you, and energy of theirs returns to them.

After you visualize this power flow ending with each person, continue by sprinkling the lavender buds onto the tablet and say:

*I am ready to move on and to heal.*

Focus your attention now on yourself. It is time for you to move forward. The damage is done. The healing must now begin. Grieve for what was lost. When you are ready to continue, take a few drops of lemon and orange essential oils and drop them onto the charcoal tablet. You should get a burst of the uplifting citrusy scent. This scent represents cleansing and purification. Visualize your energy getting an uplifting and cleansing purification treatment from the energy of the oils. Say:

*I am purified.*
*I am cleansed.*
*I am whole.*

Allow the candles to burn all the way down, incinerating the ties that bind them together as they go. Use the time it takes for any more meditative work you would like to do with this. When you are done and your candles extinguished, close your ritual as normal.

Remember: At some point during this, you may have some twine go up in flames a bit as the candles burn down.

The sand should keep anything from getting out of control but always keep a close eye on it and a little extra moon water on hand in case of an emergency.

## Energy Raising Ritual for a Cause

Need good vibes before a peaceful protest? Are you getting ready for a charity walk or 5K run? Launching a letter-writing campaign? Planning to write and promote a new petition? You can use this adaptable ritual for any supportive, community-centered event. It does not matter which cause you are working with; use this ritual to build energy and set your intentions! This ritual is not about the event itself; it is all about raising energy *for* the event.

This energy raising is not only intended for political or community-service-based projects but can be performed before a wedding or handfasting ceremony, for a baby shower, to kick off a parade, to honor the opening of a new community park, or even at the start of a pride-themed event, such as a Pagan pride festival.

There is a lot of preparation needed for this ritual; however, it is completely customizable to suit your needs. For versatility, this is designed for both solitary practices and group-based workings.

This is a two-part working. In the first part, we will design and create energy raising shakers to use in the energy raising process. This is an art project that can be a ritualistic experience itself. You can call upon your guides, meditate beforehand, create sacred space, raise energy, and enchant and charge the tools and materials that you will be using.

The materials listed here are all optional; there is no wrong way to make an energy raising shaker. For this project you can be as creative as you like! Use the materials that are available to you or think outside of the box and try something new! This is a great project for recycling too—you can use empty tea bottles, old vitamin or prescription bottles, a leftover Pringles can, or a milk jug. Search for any kind of unique container and experiment with different shapes, sizes, and textures.

For this project you will need:

* Empty container that can be sealed (Cardboard salt cans work great!)
* Masking tape
* Markers or paint and paintbrushes
* Various dried beans, small pebbles, and other small, noisy items

To begin, you will want to remove all labels from the salt cylinder or whatever container you choose to use. Open up the top and fill the container with any small items that can make noise. For this working, we used various dried beans and small pebbles. Everyone can create their own combinations for unique sounds due to the differences in weight and mass.

In addition to beans and pebbles, you can fill your shakers with other items such as small bells or beads. Crystal chips can be charged under the full moon and add power to the shaker. Allspice increases energy while cinnamon chips draw in warmth and prosperity. A pinch of lavender promotes peace and harmony. Be careful to only add a pinch if working with herbs—too much will dull the sound of the shaker.

Once you have added all your chosen items to the shaker, seal the opening tightly and cover it with masking tape to avoid an accidental opening during use. In this next step, use paint, markers, or any other crafting tools to decorate your shaker. Some materials may be more difficult to paint, so you may want to cover the shaker in construction paper, recycled newspaper, or even masking tape before you begin the decorating process.

You can design your shaker however you like. Choose any colors, designs, or symbols that you feel best align with your intentions. You can add additional crafting items such as feathers or pictures reinforced with a craft sealer like Mod Podge. Think about the cause you intend to raise energy for and customize your energy raising shaker to suit the theme. Preparing for a pride festival? Add symbols that you associate with pride, such as a rainbow!

Creating your own sigils is a great way to customize and create a unique design while also adding power to your new tool. Sigils are pictorial signatures designed by practitioners to manifest their intentions. When you create your own sigil, you set your intention into a symbol that is unique and special to you. Sigils are often personal, but groups with a shared purpose can utilize the same sigils to connect their intentions to each other. Sigils can be made in advance or created intuitively at the time of the working.

In addition to sigils, there are many runes from Norse traditions that would be appropriate to use in this project. When working with runes, you may first want to draw the rune on a separate piece of paper to practice the design. Runes can be energetically activated through meditation or by closing your eyes and focusing on the intention. Multiple runes can be used at once on the same shaker. Additionally, you can create your own bind runes by drawing two or more runes directly on top of each other, creating a unique rune. Bind runes fuse the intentions of the two separate runes into one symbol for increased power.

Below is a list of nine runes that can be used for your energy raising shaker or fused together to create custom bind runes.

| | |
|---|---|
| ᚠ | Fehu (fey-who) is commonly interpreted with ties to luck, success, abundance, and gratitude. |
| ᚢ | Uruz (oo-rooze) is a symbol of strength, ambition, perseverance, and inspiration. |
| ᚨ | Ansuz (ahn-sooze) represents divine communication, spiritual awakening, and inspiration. |
| ᚦ | Thurisaz (thoo-ree-sahz) incurs protection, good fortune, and guidance. |
| ᚲ | Kenaz (kane-awze) inspires creativity, illumination, and revelations, and is commonly used in bind runes, as it adds strength and power. |
| ᚹ | Wunjo (woon-yo) raises good vibes and attracts prosperity and good outcomes. |
| ᛉ | Eihwaz (ay-wahz) invokes spiritual enlightenment and personal development, and enhances intentions and overcoming challenges and obstacles. |
| ᛋ | Sowilo (so-wee-lo) is used to boost energy, achieve goals, increase motivation, encourage vitality, and bring intentions to life. |
| ᛞ | Dagaz (dah-gaz) represents creativity and enlightenment. |

Once you have finished designing your energy raising shaker and the paint has dried, it is time to move on to part two of this working: raising the energy.

There are many ways to raise energy. Focus on your intentions of support, compassion, unity, and universal love as you dance, chant, sing, drum, and shake that shaker every which way—or rather, every *witch* way.

A great way to build energy and add power to this working is by using music. You can use any songs that align with your intentions and hold a positive and supportive message. Choose something that is upbeat and builds in rhythm.

You can create your own customized playlist using your favorite music streaming service. If you like to use Spotify, we have created a free public playlist that can be found by searching "Community Energy Raising" featuring all of these songs listed below. This playlist can be played while designing the shakers as well as during the energy raising. The playlist has a slow build and increases in power with each song until the culmination of the finale, so these songs raise energy just as you do.

## COMMUNITY ENERGY RAISING PLAYLIST
* "Earth Air Fire Water" by Lila
* "Element Chant" by Spiral Rhythm
* "There is No Time" by Kellianna
* "We Are the Fire" by Ruth Barrett

* "We Are the Rising Sun" by Reclaiming
* "Elemental Children of the Earth" by Shining Wheel Pagan Chorus
* "Firebird's Child" by S. J. Tucker
* "Journey (Prelude)" by Crow Women
* "Full Height of Our Power" by Kellianna

As each song plays, allow yourself to truly feel the music. Raise energy by shaking the shaker like a rattle, dance, move in whatever way you choose. If you know the words, sing along. Sing along even if you don't know the words—many of these songs are repetitive, as they resemble chants, and are easy to learn.

If you do not have access to streaming music, or if you simply want to use another method, there are many chants that you can use to raise energy. Just rattle the shaker to the beat of the chants as you repeat the words at least three times over. Here are a few simple chants for groups to get you started:

*Standing in a circle*
*Hand to hand, heart to heart*
*Our intentions we do impart!*

*We rise, we rise, we rise*
*We build, we build, we build*
*Together, together, together!*

*Firelight, burning bright*
*Our energy is full tonight!*

Chanting and incantations can be used for a solitary energy raising as well. Here are a couple alternatives for chanting as a single person:

*Firelight, burning bright*
*My energy is full tonight!*

*My energy rises with the sun.*
*My intention builds with strength and power.*

*I am the change.*
*I am dawning.*

As your energy builds, focus on your intentions of positivity, support, compassion, and universal love, and send those intentions out into the world.

## Ritual to Heal Community Divide

There is no denying there is plenty of division in our world right now, on many different levels. While we tend to blame politics for the divide, the truth is, the divide is not caused by politics at all. That is a scapegoat used to not take responsibility for one's actions. The true source of the division we are seeing is a difference of ethics and belief systems clashing. One side fears losing their expected power and the control they have retained for years, while the other side demands that equality and the right to life, liberty, and the pursuit of happiness be applied to all, not the few. We passed the lines of politics a long time ago. This isn't about how we spend tax money; for many, it has become a matter of life or death. This is not political. This is ethical.

How do we heal a community after such great division? Slowly. This type of division will never heal 100 percent, and it isn't realistic to think it will. Zealots and extremists make the world a difficult place for many. Denying their existence is a disservice to our communities. Ignoring problems do not make them go away. There is no easy fix to the situation we are in, but we can send healing energies to assist. While a love-filled, hate-free world may be the perfect utopia, I think we all know it is a bit unrealistic. What isn't unrealistic is to raise and send healing compassionate energies out into a community to help it heal.

We can apply the concept of the shadow self to society as well as to the individual. There are dark components of society that need to be healed. When we work with our own shadow self, we know to listen to the expert on who we are—ourself. When we work on healing our society, it is imperative we educate ourselves from reliable sources of information. Opinions on social media are not reliable sources of information. Facts are verifiable. Opinions are not. Healing based on misinformation is not healing. It's continuing harm. Misinformation is dangerous and can be deadly. Be sure you understand what intentions you are working with and what energy you are sending out.

This ritual can be done on your own, but of course, getting a group of likeminded people together to help would increase the energy and power. The previous playlist can also be used here. In fact, these two rituals can be used in conjunction. You can use the energy raising ritual to support your cause of sending healing energy to the community.

This ritual will require a bit of advance work to prepare your altar. Find images or other representations of positive, healing, community energy. This may include things such as the scales of justice, a pride flag, or a surgical mask, but it may also include things like pictures of a local park filled with happy families or a playbill from a community theater. Brainstorm examples of positive community energy. If a group will be performing this ritual, each participant should contribute with items for the altar.

Safely decorate the altar with candles. Black candles can be used to absorb negative energy and define boundaries. Blue and green candles can be added for healing energies. Brown candles are for stability, justice, and integrity. Orange candles can be included for energy, courage, pride, and success, and to help open communication. Add pink candles to call upon the energies of compassion, honor, and peace. Finally, white candles represent cleansing, healing, and truth. If you are working with a group, each person could be responsible for providing a different color. You will want the altar placed in the center of your group with everyone circled around it.

Your altar will need a fireproof container to burn the incense mixture you will create. You will add self-lighting charcoal tablets to the bottom to burn your incense. This container should have some type of handle so once the incense is added, you will be able to pick up the container and spread the smoke all around the altar and immediate area. Again, if you are working with a group, each participant should provide an item for the incense. You will combine them all together and use a mortar and pestle to grind and blend them. In a group working, each person should take a turn with the pestle.

For the incense, you may use any combination of the following:

* Allspice for increasing energy
* Bay laurel for strength, good fortune, and success
* Blessed thistle for strength and vitality
* Borage for domestic peace, courage, and to lift spirits
* Catnip for happiness, courage, and power
* Celandine to break oppressive chains and free depressive mindsets
* Chamomile for peace, tranquility, healing, and reducing stress
* Chili pepper for energy

* Cinnamon for healing, happiness, success, love, and warmth
* Dragon's blood to banish negative forces and to amplify the power
* Eucalyptus for healing, cleansing, and warding off evil
* Fennel for healing, vitality, strength, and confidence
* Frankincense for purifying, cleansing, and manifesting
* Hibiscus for joy and happiness
* Hyssop for cleansing and lightening vibrations
* Juniper berries for good health and positive energy
* Lavender for healing, peace, and mental well-being
* Meadowsweet for peace, happiness, balance, and harmony
* Myrrh for peace and to enhance the power of the working
* Nettle leaf to block negativity
* Passionflower for health, happiness, and harmony

* Peppermint to clear negative energy and to increase vibrations
* Sandalwood for healing, clearing away negativity, manifesting, and aiding the flow of energy
* Witches burr to add power

In group work, preparing the altar and incense together allows everyone to contribute their energy to the ritual. The incense can be placed in a bowl on the altar near the fireproof container with the charcoal tablets.

Your altar should also include representations of each of the elements. Deity statues are, of course, always welcome.

When your altar is completely set up, everyone may take a place in a circle around it. Because we are working to combine energies together and amplify each other's power, each person will say the ritual in unison. No one person or voice is the leader. They are all intermingled together as one. If you are by yourself, use the "I" and "me" pronouns. If in a group, use forms of "we." For brevity, the ritual is written in first person only.

Begin by facing east:

> *I call upon the east and the power of air.*
> *Lend your power to this rite,*
> *Carry my energy on beams of light.*

Turn to face the south:

*I call upon the south and the power of fire.*
*Lend your power to this rite,*
*With flames of energy throughout the night.*

Turn to face west:

*I call upon the west and the power of water.*
*Lend your power to this rite,*
*With waves of energetic truth and right.*

Turn to face north:

*I call upon the north and the power of earth.*
*Lend your power to this rite,*
*Then soothe me with your grounding might.*

Turn to face the altar:

*This energy I raise [today/ tonight]*
*I send into the universe.*
*I send it into my community on every scale,*
*From my local neighborhood, to my city, my state,*
*my country.*
*My planet. My world. My home.*
*We must be healed.*
*We must heal the earth.*

Take some of the incense and sprinkle it gently over the lit charcoal tablets. You want enough to create a good smoke but not enough to smother the embers. (If you are doing this in a group, each person will take turns adding a pinch.) Safely pick up the container by the handle and gently move it all around the altar in front of you, spreading the smoke all around it. You may use a feather to help waft the smoke if you wish. Walk around the altar with the container; as you disperse the smoke, say:

> *My energy combines with thee,*
> *To fill my community with positivity.*

Continue this chant as each person takes their turn wafting the smoke.

If you completed the energy building ritual first, you already have a nice reserve of energy to call upon. Use this chant to continue building and releasing positive energy through the air. Visualize the qualities of the herbs in their energy forms as they are carried away in the smoke. Emanate your own energy to combine with these energies in a way that works for you. While I often visualize energy pouring out from my dominant hand, I have on occasion felt it shoot out the top of my head. You do what works for you. You do not need to worry about working the energy into a climax with one big release; you are focusing instead on a steady supply of positive, happy thoughts pumping into the universe. Continue until you feel the drain. You are giving some of your positive energy to the universe. You will feel drained.

When you are ready to finish, say:

*I give this energy willingly,*
*I share my hope for peace, for love, for charity.*
*So mote it be.*

Face the north and say:

*I thank the north and power of earth for*
*your energies.*
*Blessings and farewell.*

Face the west and say:

*I thank the west and power of water for*
*your energies.*
*Blessings and farewell.*

Face the south and say:

*I thank the south and power of fire for*
*your energies.*
*Blessings and farewell.*

Face the east and say:

*I thank the east and power of air for your energies.*
*Blessings and farewell.*

Always remember, if you are performing a ritual in a public location, ensure you not only have permission, but also that you leave the area as you found it, if not in better condition. Do not leave altar items out in a way for them to be considered litter.

## Ritual to Send Empathy and Compassion

No matter your political beliefs or affiliations, this nonpartisan ritual can be used to send empathy and compassion to our elected leaders and encourage them to express these traits themselves as they lead our country.

For this working you will need:

* A pink candle
* A safety pin
* A lighter or matches
* Olive oil
* Lavender
* Chamomile

Before you begin this ritual, you will need to prepare the pink candle. Take the safety pin and carve the word "empathy" on one side of the candle and "compassion" on the other side. Next, you will dress the candle using the olive oil, lavender, and chamomile. Olive oil is specifically used in this candle dressing as a symbol of peace and unity. Rub the oil all over the candle, avoiding contact with the wick. The lavender and chamomile should be sprinkled or rubbed onto the candle to bring in peace, tranquility, healing, and harmony. (The olive oil should help the herbs stick to the candle.)

When you are ready to begin, call upon your guides, deities, the power of the universe, and so on. Set your intentions by closing your eyes and imagining a light pink energy glowing from the candle. Focus on feelings of love, empathy, compassion, peace, and unity, and send these feelings to the candle, energetically charging it with your intention. Once your candle feels appropriately charged, open your eyes, light the wick, and speak your intention by saying:

*You have been elected into a position of power*
*And now I call upon you in this hour.*
*It is time to release selfishness and greed*
*And use your power to help those in need.*

As the wick burns, send the pink energy outward and confidently recite the following incantation nine times:

*I send you kindness, compassion, empathy, unity*
*And a desire to help improve our community.*

Allow the candle to burn fully as you focus on your intention. If you are strapped for time or working with a candle too large to burn all at once, then allow it to burn an hour a day, each day until the candle has been fully burnt. Reaffirm your intentions every time you relight the candle.

# Ritual to Heal the Environment

Nature-based practices focus on working with and honoring the earth. This planet is our only home, and it is important that we take care of the environment. Pollution and deforestation wreak havoc on the environment. The land is being stripped of resources that are vital to a thriving ecosystem. There are many ways to help heal the environment using both mundane and magical means. This ritual combines a metaphysical ritual with a laborious mundane task to heal the earth energetically with witchery as well as physically by planting more trees.

As this is a planting ritual, you will need access to gardening space. This ritual can be done as a tree planting project for a local community park or used to add more greenery to your own backyard. If neither of these options are accessible for you, this ritual can still be completed using a potted plant kept in your own home. Another option is repeating this ritual with multiple potted plants to give away as gifts to friends, family, neighbors, and coworkers.

The type of plant you use for this ritual is entirely up to you, but it is best to use plants that are specifically known for their air purifying properties.

If using this ritual to plant greenery in public spaces, it is important to make sure that you are not planting an invasive species and that you have permission from the appropriate authorities. It is also important to choose to plant something that is native to the local habitat to avoid damaging the local ecosystem. Your local conservation district is a great resource to get you started.

For this working you will need:

* A tree sapling or other sprouted plant

* Access to soil

* Gardening tools, such as a shovel

* Moon water (prepared in advance)

* Watering can

This ritual can be performed as a solitary practice or practiced with a group working together. It can be repeated every time you do some gardening or planting. Use this ritual for one potted plant or for a hundred planted trees—the choice is yours.

Gather your materials, call upon your guides, and dig your hole. Place your tree sapling or other sprouted plant in the hole. As you fill the soil back in, close your eyes for a moment. Focus your intentions on growth and healing. Send this energy into the earth as you recite:

*Here I plant new life within the earth*
*To help heal the environment and all it's worth.*

Open your eyes, finish filling any spots that need to be filled, and pat the dirt three times before watering it. If you are planting more than one thing at a time, you can choose to do all the watering all at once. When you are ready, water what you have planted with the moon water as you recite:

> *Bless the earth, bless this soil,*
> *Bless this [tree/sprout] for which I toil.*

It is important to take special care of the new life you have planted. This ritual can be reinforced monthly by using freshly charged moon water to hydrate the plants while reciting the blessing incantation.

Remember, we always want to back up our magical workings in the mundane world. What needs does your community have? What can you do to make your community a better, brighter place? No action is too big, nor too small. If we all work together to do our part, the workload becomes lighter and easier to handle. None of us are an island unto ourselves. We live, work, play, and worship in communities with other people. We must learn how to do it in a way that ensures safety and opportunity for all.

# Conclusion

*Spells for Good Times* has been a much-needed passion project for both of us. Writing this book allowed us to look within and shine the light on our own lives. We reflected on our own experiences, evaluated our responses to the hardships and chaos faced in our daily lives, and discovered inspiration in the world around us. This has been a cathartic process for both of us, and we impart all we have learned on to you. Many of these spells and rituals have come from our own personal practices, which have helped us to heal, grow, and create brighter and more abundant lives. We are grateful for the chance to share them with you.

We hope *Spells for Good Times* has given you the tools needed to build a brighter future for yourself and those around you and in your community. We hope the spells, rituals, affirmations, meditations, prayers, and journal writings included here gave you the power and insight to build up your confidence and instill within you a sense of peace and improved self-worth.

We would like to take this opportunity to thank you for reading this book. Most importantly, we thank you for allowing us a place on your path to self-discovery and healing. We wish you luck as you continue forward on your journey. Remember to live with compassion for yourself as well as others and return to these spells and rituals as needed.

Be sure to find us on social media under Kerri Connor Author (or KerriConnor.com) and for Krystle under Crescent Sapphire (https://direct.me/krystlehope).

*Laissez les bon temps rouler!*

# To Write to the Author

If you wish to contact the author or would like more information about this book, please write to the author in care of Llewellyn Worldwide Ltd. and we will forward your request. Both the author and publisher appreciate hearing from you and learning of your enjoyment of this book and how it has helped you. Llewellyn Worldwide Ltd. cannot guarantee that every letter written to the author can be answered, but all will be forwarded. Please write to:

Kerri Connor
℅ Llewellyn Worldwide
2143 Wooddale Drive
Woodbury, MN 55125-2989

Please enclose a self-addressed stamped envelope for reply,
or $1.00 to cover costs. If outside the U.S.A., enclose
an international postal reply coupon.

Many of Llewellyn's authors have websites with additional information and resources. For more information, please visit our website at http://www.llewellyn.com